THOMAS HEINSER

WILLIAM SEARS, M.D., and MARTHA SEARS, R.N., are the pediatrics experts to whom American parents are increasingly turning for advice and information on all aspects of pregnancy, birth, childcare, and family nutrition. Dr. Sears was trained at Harvard Medical School's Children's Hospital and Toronto's Hospital for Sick Children, the largest children's hospital in the world. He has practiced pediatrics for nearly thirty years and currently serves as a medical and parenting consultant to *Baby Talk* and *Parenting* magazines. Martha Sears is a registered nurse, certified childbirth educator, and breastfeeding consultant. The Searses are the parents of eight children.

More information about the Searses can be found at www.SearsParenting.com and www.AskDrSears.com.

Feeding the Picky Eater

America's Foremost Baby and
Childcare Experts Answer the Most
Frequently Asked Questions

William Sears, M.D.,
and Martha Sears, R.N.

Little, Brown and Company
BOSTON | NEW YORK | LONDON

First Edition

The information herein is not intended to replace the services of trained health professionals. You are advised to consult with your child's health-care professional with regard to matters relating to your child's health, and in particular matters that may require diagnosis or medical attention.

Library of Congress Cataloging-in-Publication Data

Sears, William, M.D.
    Feeding the picky eater / by William Sears and Martha Sears. — 1st ed.
        p. cm. — (Sears parenting library)
    ISBN 0-316-77677-7
    1. Children — Nutrition — Psychological aspects — Miscellanea.
    2. Food preferences in children — Miscellanea.   I. Sears, Martha.
    II. Title.
    RJ206.S493 2001
    649'.3 — dc21   00-0455140

10 9 8 7 6 5 4 3 2 1

Book design and text composition by L&G McRee

Printed in the United States of America

Introduction

Many kids ago we learned that children do what they do simply because they are designed that way. For example, toddlers are picky eaters because they have tiny tummies, about the size of their fist. The next time you put a plate full of food next to your picky toddler, compare it with the size of her fist, and you'll see why most of it goes uneaten.

There are developmental reasons that children between one and three years pick and poke at their food. After a year of rapid growth, tripling their birth weight by one year, toddlers gain weight much more slowly. Naturally, they need less food. Because of their tiny tummies, toddlers like to graze and nibble on favorite foods throughout the day. Eating many meals spaced throughout the day (what we call "mini-meals") is nutritionally correct for young children.

Throughout this book we will give you tips straight from the Sears family kitchen on how to get the most nutritious foods into your infant or young child with the fewest headaches. You will learn why your baby may prefer the taste of commercial baby food, why some formulas cause gastrointestinal problems, and how to wean your baby effectively from the bottle to a cup. You will learn how to prepare a toddler nibble tray, create edible art to make veggies more attractive, and serve brainy breakfasts on those rushed, harried mornings when you find it challenging to give your child the best nutritional start. As you learn these quick-and-easy tips to minimize mealtime hassles, you will make eating fun and nutritious.

More than two thousand years ago, Hippocrates, the founder of medicine, said, "Let food be thy medicine." I've seen this truth confirmed again and again over my almost thirty years as a pediatrician: The healthiest children are the ones who eat the most nutritious food. Learning how children eat has helped us realize that our job as parents of eight is to buy the right food, prepare it nutritiously, and serve it creatively. The rest is up to our children!

Now let the following pages show you how to shape the habits and tastes of your children as they learn to eat more nutritious foods and develop lifelong healthy eating habits.

WILLIAM SEARS, M.D., and MARTHA SEARS, R.N.

Feeding
the Picky Eater

☙

Solid Food for Different Ages and Stages

Q *Is there a rule about what foods babies should eat at different stages? I'm afraid of giving my fourteen-month-old any solid food for fear she will choke. But I want her to learn about different tastes. How do I know what is age-appropriate for her?*

A When, what, and how much solid food varies greatly from baby to baby. Here are some general guidelines to follow:

- *Six to nine months.* Babies rarely need solid food under six months, but some babies enjoy experimenting with different textures as early as four months. Sometime between four and six months watch for these readiness signs: Baby mooches or reaches for food on your plate or mimics you while you are eating by opening her mouth wide. She may even grab your spoon or reach toward it—this is a mixed message, though, since baby may just want to play with the utensil in the food and not eat the food. Once you feel your baby is ready and willing, begin with a fingertip covered with mashed bananas (the texture and taste are closest to mother's milk and formula). If the test dose of banana comes right back at you with a disapproving grimace, wait a couple of weeks and try again. If the banana taste is accompanied with an approving smile, you can gradually increase the amount of bananas and move on to rice cereal.

Every week or so you can then increase the amount and variety of foods. Try, for example, sweet potatoes, carrots, squash, pears, applesauce, mashed potatoes, avocados, peaches, prunes, barley cereal, and teething biscuits.

- *Nine to twelve months.* At this age, give more "melt in the mouth" foods, such as rice cakes, pasta (nonwheat first), tofu, and yogurt. Introduce other fruits and vegetables, such as papaya, peas, refried beans, apricots, and also egg yolks. You can also introduce pureed meats, such as lamb, veal, and poultry.

- *One to two years.* Now you can introduce whole milk, whole eggs, whole wheat cookies, fish (tuna and salmon), bagels, melons, mangos, kiwis, spinach, broccoli, and all the whole-grain cereals and whole-grain crackers. Dips such as avocado and yogurt are favorites from eighteen months to two years.

Remember, your goal is to introduce your baby to a variety of textures and tastes, not to fill her up at each meal. It's best to introduce small dollops of new foods. Tiny babies have tiny tummies, so be especially cautious about feeding her large amounts of new foods until she approves of the taste and her intestines approve of the new food.

To reduce the chance of choking, do not give the following foods to young children:

- Hard candy
- Hot dog chunks (cut them lengthwise in strips)
- Glob of raisins
- Cherries with pits
- Whole grapes
- Whole olives
- Nuts
- Popcorn
- Raw apples, carrots, pears, and green beans

Also, follow these rules to ensure safe eating habits:

- Be careful of big globs of food, such as golf-ball-size, pasty white bread or fingerfuls of peanut butter.
- Watch out for chunks of food that are about the size of a child's windpipe, such as hot dog and meat chunks.
- Have a sit-down-and-eat rule rather than let your child run around the house with a handful of snacks.
- Slice apples, grapes, and pears into strips.
- Feed your child cooked fruits and vegetables until she is about three years old. Once the molars appear (between two and three years of age), children can usually mash chunks of food and safely swallow them. But even when she is three years of age, it's best not to let your child stuff big globs of chunky food into her mouth.

One of the main goals when it comes to childhood nutrition is to shape your child's tastes by exposing her to a variety of different tastes and textures and presenting different foods creatively.

❧

Resolving Constipation with Food

Q *My two-year-old son is a picky eater and detests fruits and vegetables. Because of this, he has trouble moving his bowels, even though we're giving him a daily doctor-recommended dose of Senokot Children's Syrup. We're also trying to encourage more fiber and vegetables in his diet. When he tries to pass his stools, he cries, screams, draws his legs into his chest, and even throws up from pushing so hard. It's been this way for nine months. Is it normal for this problem to persist for so long? What else can we do? And are we missing something medical?*

A Constipation can be a painful cycle. Your baby's bowel movements become hard and painful, usually because of dietary changes. This causes him to hold them in, which makes them harder and more difficult to pass. Over time, the bowel muscle weakens, and that further aggravates the problem. Remember that it takes about six weeks of stool softening for the bowel muscle to regain its strength.

Eating the right foods and drinking plenty of fluids can help resolve constipation. Try to increase the amount of fluids in his diet, making sure that he gets at least 32 ounces a day. In addition to milk, formula, and water, try prune, pear, or apricot nectar. Nectar has more pulp and therefore more fiber than strained juice.

Add fiber-rich foods to your toddler's diet, such as whole-grain breads, graham crackers, bran cereals, and high-fiber vegetables, like broccoli, peas, and beans. Make a puree of high-fiber fruits to spread on whole-grain bread. Use the four P's (prunes, pears, plums, and peaches) to make the puree.

If he doesn't like to eat fresh fruits, make him a daily smoothie using seasonal fruits (see below). Strawberries, blueberries, and papaya are excellent fiber sources, and papaya is especially intestines-friendly. Add 2 teaspoons of flax oil, a nutritious supplement available at your health food store that contributes to stool softening.

You will need to watch for his "about to go" signals of squatting and straining. You may have to ease the passage of hard stools by using a daily glycerin suppository (available over the counter) for a few days. But once the stools are softer, you will find that he will not refuse to pass them.

Sears Family Child-Pleasing Recipes

Smoothie

1 handful frozen strawberries
1 handful frozen blueberries
1 frozen banana, diced
½ papaya
8 oz. frozen yogurt

1 tbsp. honey
1 tbsp. flax oil
1 serving protein powder
8 oz. milk, juice, or soy beverage

Blend the ingredients to the consistency of a milkshake and serve.

Zucchini Pancakes

½ small zucchini, finely grated
1 egg
2 tbsp. whole wheat flour
1 tsp. baking powder

Blend the ingredients to make a batter. Cook the pancakes. Top with a pat of butter and some jam for an extra treat.

✍

Short-Order-Cook Syndrome

Q *My three-year-old turns her nose up at any dinner I fix for our family. I try to keep the meal balanced and include something she will enjoy. But no matter what I fix, she pushes her plate away. I get so frustrated, I end up catering to her whim at the moment—whether it means fixing PB&J or pizza. Am I a pushover? What should I do?*

A Feeding children is a combination of good nutrition and creative marketing. You don't have to be a short-order cook and cater to your child's every eating whim. Here are some tricks from the Sears family kitchen to put more nutrition and less hassle into getting your child to eat. Once your child gains appreciation for good food, you will not have to resort to all these tricks.

Dip It!

Young children think that immersing foods in a tasty dip is fun and delightfully messy. Some favorites include:

- Guacamole (without the strong spices)
- Yogurt
- Refried bean dip
- Cream cheese
- Cottage cheese or tofu dip
- Pureed fruits and vegetables
- Healthy salad dressings
- Fruit juice–sweetened ketchup

Spread It!

Besides dipping, toddlers like to spread (or smear). Show her how to use a small, blunt butter knife to spread peanut butter, cheese, and fruit concentrate on crackers, toast, or rice cakes.

Top It!

Put nutritious familiar favorites on top of new and less desirable foods. Favorite toddler toppings are:

• Yogurt
• Light cream cheese
• Melted cheese
• Guacamole
• Tomato sauce
• Apple sauce
• Peanut butter

Drink It!

If you can't get your child to eat her meal, perhaps you can get her to drink it. Make a smoothie together (see pages 7–8). Oftentimes we got our children to eat their meals through a straw when they were in the "refusal to eat" stage.

Create It!

As with fine cuisine served in a good restaurant, presentation is important. Make veggie art. Create colorful plate faces with olive eyes, tomato ears, mushroom noses, and bell pepper mustaches. Zucchini pancakes make a nutritious head to which you can add pea eyes, a carrot nose, shredded cheese head, and a green bean smile. Try edible art, such as a cereal necklace. String O-shaped cereal and dried apple slices on a piece of string or dental floss. Try a cottage cheese cone. Make "pretty pizzas" using pita bread or English muffins sliced in half. Spread on the tomato sauce, then make a face or design with cheese triangles, sliced olives, or whatever toppings she likes, and warm it up.

Plant It!

Plant a garden with your child. Let her help care for the plants, harvest vegetables, and wash and prepare them. Children are more likely to eat what they helped grow and prepare.

Have Fun with It!

Enjoy some fun mother-daughter kitchen time. Make whole wheat oatmeal cookies. Teach her how to spread the peanut butter and fruit juice–sweetened jellies on whole wheat bread. Show your child how to use cookie cutters to create edible designs out of foods she likes, such as whole wheat bread, thin meat slices, or cooked lasagne noodles. Give your little assistant fun jobs, such as washing and tearing lettuce, scrubbing potatoes, and stirring batter. Put pancake batter in a squeeze bottle and guide her hands as she squeezes the batter on the griddle in fun shapes, such as hearts, numbers, letters, or even her name.

Organize It!

Finally, give your toddler her own shelf space in the refrigerator. Reserve a low shelf to provide all of your toddler's favorite and nutritious foods and drinks. Nibbling on nutritious foods during the day mellows a toddler's erratic moods by encouraging her to eat when she's hungry.

ॐ

Preventing Food Poisoning

Q *Every time I turn on the news, I hear about another outbreak of* E. coli *or* Salmonella. *How can I protect my kids from food poisoning? Is food poisoning more of a threat during the summer, when food sits outside at barbecues and hamburgers are often served?*

A Despite news reports, the majority of children never experience a case of food poisoning that causes more than a stomachache. However, when food poisoning strikes in a child under five, the symptoms can be more severe.

The two most common microorganisms that taint food are the bacteria *Salmonella* and some strains of *Escherichia coli (E. coli)*. Both produce similar symptoms: diarrhea, vomiting, abdominal cramping, and sometimes a fever.

Responsible for more cases of food poisoning than any other bacteria, *Salmonella* is found in raw or undercooked meats or poultry, unrefrigerated or cracked eggs, unrefrigerated dairy products, fish from *Salmonella*-contaminated waters, unpasteurized milk, and sometimes fruits and vegetables.

There are hundreds of strains of *E. coli*. While most are harmless, a few can produce powerful toxins. Meat, especially ground beef, is the most common breeding ground for *E. coli*. The bacteria live in the intestines of healthy cattle, and toxic strains can contaminate the meat during slaughter. Grinding the beef spreads the microorganism throughout the meat.

Improper cooking and food storage are the primary culprits. Poor hygienic habits while handling food, such as not washing hands before preparing food, can spread foodborne microorganisms. Also, caregivers of babies can spread the disease if they don't wash their hands after every diaper change, since the bacteria may be carried in stools. Summertime living encourages the spread of food poisoning, as food left out in the sun can become contaminated. Undercooked burgers are also a source of food poisoning.

To prevent food poisoning, take these steps to protect your kids:

- Cook food thoroughly. When cooking burgers or ordering them at fast-food outlets, make sure that they're served well done. Check that the meat is gray or brown throughout, not pink. Cook chicken until its juices run clear rather than bloody when it is pierced with a fork.

The meat should be white throughout, with no traces of pink.

- Don't let uncooked food sit at room temperature if it needs refrigeration. After grocery shopping, refrigerate food as soon as you get home. When cooking, put ingredients away immediately after you use them. Defrost food in the refrigerator, not on your countertop.
- Store uncooked meats in a compartment in your refrigerator that is separate from produce and other food.
- Adhere to hygienic guidelines when preparing food, especially chicken or other high-risk food: Wash your hands, countertops, cutting boards, and all cooking utensils with hot, soapy water between each preparation step. Don't use the same knife to cut other foods that you use for meat or chicken.
- Don't store cooked meats, chicken, eggs, or other high-risk food in the same container that you stored them in when they were raw, unless you first wash the container thoroughly in hot, soapy water.
- Keep perishable food out of the sun at picnics and barbecues. Store meats, salads, mayonnaise, eggs, sandwiches, and dairy products in a cooler placed in the shade until you are ready to serve them. Don't eat food that has been sitting out for more than four hours.
- Wash vegetables thoroughly.
- Both when cooking and when dining out, be wary of sauces, dressings, and dishes that could contain raw contaminated food. These include hollandaise sauce, Caesar and other salad dressings, homemade ice cream, homemade mayonnaise, cookie dough, and frostings.
- Prepare a sandwich the night before for a child who goes

to school or day care. Store it in the refrigerator, then put it in your child's lunch right before he trots out the door. A chilled sandwich gives germs a less friendly breeding ground. Remind your child not to leave the lunch in a hot place, especially out in the sun. If your child carries a lunch box, wash it out after each use. If you pack lunches in paper bags, use a clean one for each lunch. If you use a recyclable fabric lunch bag and it has a plastic liner, wash the liner. If the bag doesn't have a lining, wash the bag after each use.

- Don't let your child swim in or drink from potentially contaminated rivers or lakes. If you are camping, boil the water for five minutes to kill the microorganisms.

If your child gets food poisoning in spite of these precautions, give him ice chips and homemade juice ice pops. Withhold all other food until his symptoms subside. Your goal is to rest your child's intestines while preventing dehydration. Food poisoning symptoms usually ease within six to eight hours. If they last longer and your child also shows signs of dehydration (less frequent urination, fewer tears when crying, a dry mouth, weight loss, and lethargy), call your doctor.

✑

Strawberry Allergy

Q *My ten-month-old son recently reacted with vom-iting and hives after eating a commercial baby food con-taining strawberries. Does this mean he'll have a more serious reaction to fresh strawberries? Should I be con-cerned about other fruits as well?*

A Strawberries contain a common food allergen that is best avoided by babies under the age of one year. The good news, however, is that infants outgrow most of their food allergies by the time they are two years old.

Subsequent ingestion of strawberries could result in a more severe allergic reaction, so avoid feeding your son strawberries for at least six more months and be sure to mention his strawberry allergy to substitute caregivers or anyone who might have occasion to feed your baby.

As a precaution, stay away from citrus fruits for a few more months. Your baby doesn't need strawberries or citrus fruits at this age. He can get all the necessary nutri-ents from a balanced diet of breast milk or formula, grains, vegetables, and less allergenic fruits (pears, applesauce, papayas, and bananas).

As your baby's intestines grow, the allergens are less likely to be absorbed through the intestines into the blood-stream. But to be on the safe side, when you give him strawberries again (at around two years of age), do it gradually. Begin with half a strawberry once a day for a few days and see what happens.

⚭

Picky Baby vs.
Formula Intolerance

Q *Our two-month-old has crying spells that last for up to an hour. During the spells, she passes gas. We recently switched from breastfeeding to bottlefeeding. The doctor says it takes a few weeks to adjust and that our baby's body is getting used to the formula. Is this correct?*

A The fact that your baby's upset began when you switched from breast milk to formula is a sign that she is allergic to the formula. Rather than continue with the same formula and run the risk of prolonged intestinal discomfort, we suggest that you experiment with various types of formulas and methods of feeding.

Baby formula contains protein and lactose, which can cause abdominal upset. So begin with formulas that vary these nutritional elements. To determine if your baby is lactose-intolerant, try a lactose-free formula for a week. If she is still gassy, she may be allergic to cow's-milk protein. If that is the case, switch to a soy-based formula (such as

Isomil or Enfamil ProSobee) for a week. If the gassiness
persists, try Alimentum or Nutramigen. Both are lactose-
free and contain predigested cow's-milk protein, which
makes them hypoallergenic. Smaller, more frequent feedings may also help your baby get used to digesting formula.

As your baby's intestines mature, the gassy stage will
pass. In the meantime, though, here are ways to relieve her
discomfort:

- *The gas pump.* Lay your baby on her back on your lap
  with her head resting on your knees and her legs pointing
  toward you. Pump her legs in a bicycling motion.
- *The colic curl.* Slide your baby's back down your chest,
  and encircle your arms under her bottom. Curl baby up,
  facing forward, with her head and back resting against
  your chest. Or try reversing the position, holding your
  baby facing you with her feet against your chest. In this
  position, you can maintain eye contact and play facial
  gesture games with your baby.
- *The tummy tuck.* Place a rolled-up cloth diaper or warm
  (not hot) water bottle wrapped in a cloth diaper under
  your baby's tummy during gas pain. To further relax a
  tense tummy, lay baby stomach-down on a cushion with
  her legs dangling over the edge, and rub her back.
- *Tummy touches.* Place the palm of your hand over your
  baby's navel and let your finger and thumb encircle her
  abdomen. Let her lean her tense abdomen against your
  warm hand.
- *The "I love U" touch.* Practice this massage with your
  baby on your lap, feet facing you. Rub some warm massage oil on your hands and knead baby's tense abdomen
  with your flattened fingers in a circular motion. Picture

an upside-down *U* on your baby's abdomen. Start with a downward stroke for the *I* on baby's left side, then massage along the upside-down *L* along the top of your baby's abdomen. Finally, massage along the upside-down *U,* stroking upward along the right, across, and down the left side.

ℒ&

Feeding a Baby Solids

Q *At four months I introduced my son to baby food, but at six months he still doesn't like it. We can barely get him to swallow a teaspoonful. I'm concerned that he's not getting enough nutrition. He still does very well on formula and isn't underweight, but how can I get him to eat baby food?*

A Babies under six months don't need solid foods for nutrition, although some may enjoy variety in their diets. The fact that your baby is gaining weight indicates that the formula is providing the nutrition he needs.

Babies refuse solid foods for several reasons. Many four-month-olds shun solids because developmentally they're not ready to swallow anything thicker than formula. They also may not like the taste. Food allergies are another reason. Even a four-month-old will refuse a food that upsets his intestines. Force-feeding a baby before his intestines are sufficiently mature sets him up for food allergies later on.

Here are some tips to help your baby make the transition to solids:

- *Watch for ready-to-eat signs.* Your baby will start reaching for the food on your plate, grabbing your spoon, looking at you hungrily, and mimicking feeding behavior, such as opening his mouth wide when you open yours to eat.
- *Start with mashed ripe bananas or rice cereal.* These foods are the least allergenic and closest to formula in taste and consistency. Place a fingertip-size serving of banana on your baby's lips and let him suck your finger. Once he's accustomed to the new taste, gradually increase the amount and thickness of the food.
- *Observe facial reactions.* If the food goes in accompanied by an approving smile, baby is ready and willing. If it comes back at you with a disapproving grimace, eliminate the food from his diet for now and try again in a couple of weeks. Pursed lips, a closed mouth, and turning the head away from an approaching spoon are all signs that your baby does not want to eat solids.
- *Don't force-feed.* Some babies eagerly take solids at four months, while others show little interest until nine to twelve months. Following your baby's cues will help him to develop a healthy attitude toward food and feeding.

☞

Introducing Baby
to a Cup

Q *My twelve-month-old baby is completely weaned, but she refuses to drink from a bottle or cup. As a result, she has been hospitalized for dehydration and a viral infection. We've tried sippy cups, straw cups, bottles, and open cups. We finally resorted to forcing liquids into her mouth by syringe. Why is she refusing to drink? How do I get her to drink?*

A After weaning, some babies have a hard time adjusting to a new suck-swallow mechanism. Babies sucking from the breast can control the flow of milk. But the faster and easier flow from a cup or bottle sometimes overwhelms an infant and conditions her to not want to drink.

Your baby needs some gradual suck-swallow retraining so that she takes in the optimal amount of fluid (16 to 24 ounces a day). Here's what we suggest:

- *Try homemade juice ice pops.* Licking a frozen Popsicle delivers small amounts of fluid gradually.
- *Experiment with various types of nipples and nipple-hole sizes.* Normally, if you hold a full bottle upside down without shaking it, the milk should drip at one drop per second. Try enlarging the nipple hole a bit using the prong of a clean fork.

- *Encourage imitation.* Capitalize on a one-year-old's eagerness to copy your behavior. When your infant sees you sipping from a cup, she may be motivated to try it, too.

- *Avoid feeding battles,* which condition a negative attitude toward drinking. Wear a happy face during feeding time to show your baby that feeding is a natural thing to do. If baby senses your anxiety about feeding, she is likely to become anxious, too. (Admittedly, this is easier said than done, since we all take feeding our babies personally, and few things bother parents more than their baby's refusal to eat.)

- *Blend milk or formula smoothies.* Smoothies (see pages 7–8) or other soupy mixtures are a great way to get more fluids into your baby. Add fresh fruit to the smoothie and experiment with various mixtures and consistencies. See if she will spoon the fluid herself.

⌨

Guidelines for
Introducing Solids

Q *My daughter is almost five months old and weighs about 15 pounds. For the past month I've been feeding her cereal, but I'm not sure I understand the schedule. How often should I feed my baby cereal—once or twice a day? She still eats five times a day and is sleeping through the night.*

A What, when, and how often to feed an infant solid foods varies from baby to baby, but here are some general guidelines:

When to Start

Most babies under six months do not need solid foods; they receive all the nutrition they need from breast milk or iron-fortified formula. Between four and six months, however, some babies show "begging for food" signs, such as making mouthing movements while watching you eat or grabbing for your food.

With new insights into infant nutrition, pediatricians recommend starting solid foods later rather than sooner. The intestinal lining isn't mature enough to absorb solids in the first few months, and giving a baby solid foods before the intestines are ready may lead to food allergies. Also, some infants become constipated from eating too much rice cereal too soon. Read your baby's tastes. If your infant enjoys solid foods, he's ready.

How Often? How Much?

Once-a-day feedings of solid food are enough for a five-month-old. Between six and seven months, you can increase to twice a day. You can feed a formula-fed infant solids at any time of the day. When breastfeeding, however, it's best to offer solids at the end of the day, when your milk supply diminishes. The amount varies according to your infant's tastes, but it's usually around 1 tablespoon of dried cereal mixed with formula or breast milk.

Progression

The progression of solids varies from baby to baby. Here are five foods our infants seemed to prefer, and the order in which we introduced them. These foods are nutritious and accepted by most five- to eight-month-olds:

- mashed, ripe bananas
- pureed pears
- rice or barley cereal
- pureed sweet potatoes
- pureed avocados

Menu Planning

Your infant will let you know when she likes certain foods and when she's had enough to eat. To test the waters, place a small dollop of a new solid on her tongue, using your fingertip or a spoon. If the morsel is devoured with an approving smile, add the food to her feeding menu. If the food quickly comes back at you, accompanied by a disapproving grimace, omit it from her current diet and try again in a month or two.

Above all, remember that feeding is about social interaction as well as nutrition delivery. Make lots of facial gestures during the "feeding game" and enjoy these special times with your baby.

ℒ&

Weaning from the Bottle

Q *Last month we weaned our two-year-old son from the bottle. He had been drinking milk from a cup during the day and taking a bottle at naptime and bedtime. Now he refuses to drink from a cup. We've tried cups with sippy straws with moderate success. I'm trying to give him other dairy products to balance his diet. Any suggestions?*

A The more children you have, the sooner you realize that it's easier to follow a child's own timetable than to adhere to a developmental calendar. There is nothing magical about turning two and giving up the bottles; some two-year-olds do it willingly and some don't. Persistent bottle use seems to bother adults more than it does children. The only time a bottle bothers a child is when sucking on a juice- or milk-filled nipple all night causes tooth decay.

Most parents find it easier to allow their toddler to take juice and milk during the day from whatever container gets the most fluid into the child with the least amount of mess. One trick we've used is to drink our mealtime fluids from sippy cups, which are available at most grocery stores. A youngster who sees Mommy and Daddy using a sippy cup will want to use one, too. The bottom line is that toddlers need at least a quart of fluid a day, which is a lot to get by cup. So if you've tried every other container without success, just return to the bottle.

Introducing the Bottle

Q *My wife is breastfeeding and pumping her own milk for our one-month-old baby. Lately, though, we have been trying to supplement breastfeeding with an occasional bottle, but the baby refuses the bottle. She becomes fussy, turns her head, pushes the bottle away, and cries. We've gotten her to take the bottle only once. We're looking for advice on how to get her started on bottlefeeding.*

A Don't expect your little gourmet to take a bottle from her breastfeeding mother. Some babies are such confirmed breastfeeders that as soon as someone offers a bottle, they click into a "what's-wrong-with-this-picture" mind-set. That's exactly what your baby is doing.

Here are some ways to get your baby to accept an occasional substitute for the breast:

- Enlist an experienced bottlefeeder, such as Grandma or another bottlefeeding mother. Once your baby learns to accept the bottle from the experienced feeder, ask Dad to take a turn at bottlefeeding.
- Hold your baby differently when you bottlefeed. Holding your baby the way she is used to being held during breastfeeding may confuse her, and she will refuse the bottle. During bottlefeeding, position your baby at a different angle and sit in a different location from the one used for breastfeeding.

- Try walking or rocking your baby while you offer the bottle. The distraction of movement may help her "settle for less."
- Heat the bottle nipple in warm water to make it more supple and breastlike. During teething time, though, some babies prefer a chilled bottle nipple.
- Avoid bottle-propping for safety's sake, and never leave baby to take her own bottle unattended.

Remember that in addition to delivering nutrition, feeding is also a social interaction. During bottlefeeding, try to connect with your baby in amusing ways that are different from her interactions during breastfeeding. Your baby will often enjoy bottlefeeding as a social event, even if she's not getting the container she prefers.

◈

Picky Baby's Sweet Tooth

Q *My nine-month-old daughter is in great health, but she's a picky eater and won't eat on her own. She refuses to hold her bottle of formula and does not like finger foods at all. I want to start her on regular food like rice and bread, but she prefers cereal and jar fruits and vegetables. I think she's developed a sweet tooth. Can you help?*

A Your baby was born with a sweet tooth! Babies prefer sweet foods, which is why breast milk is sweet. Your baby's preference for cereal, fruits, and vegetables should be welcomed because these foods provide a nutritious balance for her formula.

One of your primary goals in introducing solid foods is to give your baby a healthy attitude about food—to help her understand that food tastes good and is fun to eat. Keep this in mind so that you don't get preoccupied with how much she eats, which might vary from day to day.

Also remember that feeding babies is part nutrition and part marketing. If you're creative and patient, you'll ease the transition.

So let's get started! Begin by putting some of your baby's food on your plate, since she might prefer that to her own bowl. And start with small amounts—a couple of teaspoons of each food, increasing the portions gradually over time.

Allow her to play with the food a bit if she wants to, as this is part of the early feeding game. Or take a fingerful of a new food and place it on the tip of your baby's tongue. If she takes the food and flashes an approving smile, continue. But if she rejects it, scratch that food for a couple of weeks and try again.

Don't worry about your daughter's unwillingness to hold her bottle. Take it as a sign that she wants you to hold her during the feeding. Remember, feeding is not only a source of nutrition but also a social interaction. At least for the first year, there should always be someone at both ends of the bottle.

ॐ

Vitamin Supplements for Breastfed Babies

Q *My baby is two months old. Our pediatrician told us to start giving her vitamin drops with iron when she was a month old. But when I try giving her the drops, she spits them up. I've read that a breastfed baby gets enough nutrients from her mother's milk, at least until she is six months old. Is this true? If not, how can I successfully give her the drops? Can I wait until she's four months old and stir the drops into her cereal, or will that make them less effective?*

A Mother Nature provides all the necessary nutrients a baby needs in mother's milk. A healthy full-term baby who is getting enough breast milk does not need iron or vitamin supplements.

The custom of giving these supplements to babies is based upon outdated information. Decades ago, when the nutritional content of breast milk was analyzed, it was found (on paper) to be low in iron and some vitamins. But new information shows that even though the iron and vitamins in breast milk may be lower in quantity, they are superior in quality. These nutrients enjoy a higher bioavailability, meaning that more of the iron and probably more of the vitamins are better absorbed in mother's milk than are those added to commercial formulas or cereal.

If your baby was premature, had a low birth weight, or does not seem to be getting enough breast milk, your doctor may recommend nutritional supplements. If your doctor is worried about your baby's iron stores, he or she may check your baby's hemoglobin, usually at your baby's nine-month checkup. But for the first six months, have confidence that your milk can provide all the nutrition your baby needs.

✑

Chubby Preschoolers

Q *My three-year-old daughter is chubby for her age. She is relatively active and eats healthy foods at home, but she also loves junk food. She gets upset when we tell her she shouldn't eat something because it's not good for her (she wants to be in control). We're concerned because obesity runs in our families.*

A The best way to teach your daughter healthy eating habits is to model them yourself. While you can't control what she eats when she is at a friend's house or at pre-school, you can strongly influence her choices by how you stock the pantry and refrigerator. Set aside a month of "pure" eating habits during which time you buy and serve only healthy foods, and make sure all family members adhere to this healthy-eating month.

Here are some other suggestions to encourage your preschooler's healthy eating habits:

* *Take her with you on a grocery run.* As you roam the aisles, read the labels out loud to her and tell her the differences between healthy foods and junk foods. For example, foods high in saturated or hydrogenated, or fake, fats are not healthy. Fake fats are potentially harmful to the body, but food manufacturers include them as flavoring tricks to entice kids to overdose on their products (think of the ad slogan "Bet you can't eat just one").

* *Teach her about feeding her body healthy foods.* Instead of telling her a particular food will make her chubby, explain that some foods become extra fat, and some don't. For example, highly sugared foods (junk sugars) are deposited as extra fat, as are foods containing high amounts of unhealthy fats, such as saturated fats and hydrogenated fats. Growing children need fats, though, so don't let the no-fat craze popular with adults cause undernutrition in your child. Instead, stick to vegetable oils, such as olive oil, flax oil, and fish oils, which provide healthy fats.

* *Spend time cooking together.* Discussing healthful eating during food preparation is more effective than making your child's eating habits a topic of mealtime discussion. Let her help you tear lettuce for the salad or toss cheese on a favorite vegetable casserole. Your child will be motivated to eat healthy meals if she helps to prepare them.

&

Toddler's Limited Diet

Q *My one-year-old daughter eats only grains, dates, and bananas. She's not coordinated enough yet to dip veggies or do her own spreading, as you have recommended. I try to introduce foods more than once, but whenever I give her vegetables she just throws them on the floor. Should I be worried about her vitamin intake? I need suggestions for "creative marketing" to get her to eat healthy.*

A One-year-olds can get most of their nutrition from milk or formula. But at this age, your infant also needs iron. If you are bottlefeeding, be sure to use an iron-fortified formula. Another rich source of iron that one-year-olds will take is iron-fortified infant rice or barley cereal.

Your infant's current diet of formula, grains, dates, and bananas seems surprisingly balanced—especially if she's thriving. To determine if your infant is eating enough, do a daily calorie count for a week. Your infant should eat an average of 40 to 50 calories per pound per day (for a 20-pound one-year-old, that's 800 to 1,000 calories a day). If your daughter drinks 30 ounces of formula every day, that alone is 600 calories.

Try these creative marketing tips:

- *Let her mooch.* Allow your daughter to sit on your lap and eat from your plate.

- *Choose palate pleasers.* Two particularly nutritious foods with a consistency one-year-olds like are sweet potatoes and avocados. Sweet potatoes are rich in beta carotene, and avocados contain healthy fats and provide the extra calories an active one-year-old needs.
- *Create a rainbow plate.* Meals with deeper and more varied food colors tend to be more nutritious. For a colorful and nutritious lunch, arrange a plate with dollops of pureed sweet potatoes, avocados, blueberries, strawberries, papayas, or broccoli.
- *Keep portions small.* A one-year-old may take only a tablespoon of a vegetable or fruit at each meal.
- *Camouflage veggies with fruit topping.* Infants are more likely to eat vegetables when they're topped with something fruity. For example, try spreading applesauce on sweet potatoes.
- *Encourage imitation.* One-year-olds love to imitate Mom and Dad. To encourage this, eat a bit of food off your baby's plate and make exaggerated facial gestures to show how yummy it is.
- *Allow grazing.* Grazing is a healthy habit that fits the life of a busy toddler because it steadies the blood sugar and stabilizes behavior. In fact, small, frequent feedings throughout the day will get more food into a child with fewer hassles.
- *Fresh is best.* As much as possible, use fresh rather than commercial baby food. One goal of infant feeding is to shape young tastes. So try to get your baby used to the taste of fresh foods.

Finally, bear in mind that many infants who are slow to

accept solids may have temporary allergies. Their bodies might be intolerant of the foods they refuse.

☙

Fussy Eater

Q *My three-and-a-half-year-old daughter is a fussy eater, and it has become a major effort to get her to eat. It takes her an hour to eat dinner, and she is always the last to finish lunch at preschool. We have to nudge her constantly to eat her food. What is the best way to approach this?*

A Eating, like sleeping, isn't something you can force your child to do. It's best not to make food a power struggle. Your preschooler may be a grazer who knows she feels better and her body works better if she nibbles frequently throughout the day with mini-meals rather than consuming three big meals. Actually, most children do better by constant nibbling and snacking. Watch for the food-mood connection. Children who graze tend to experience fewer blood-sugar swings and that means fewer mood swings.

Try setting a good example by practicing good eating habits yourself and encourage healthy grazing by packing nutritious snacks for your daughter to eat midmorning and midafternoon while at school.

Encourage her to eat nutrient-dense foods. These are foods that pack a lot of nutrition in a small number of calories. Avocados, nut butter, yogurt, tofu, cheese, egg, turkey, and fish are good choices. Put small portions of food on her plate and offer refills as desired. Large portions overwhelm some children.

Make food fun. Encourage your daughter to help you bake cookies and cakes and pack them with a lot of nutritious ingredients. (Try using fruit concentrate instead of sugar and use whole wheat flour.) Children are more likely to eat what they help make. If you really want to go the extra mile, plant a small garden. Children are even more likely to eat what they help grow.

Encourage dipping. Kids love to dip. You can make a nutritious dip out of yogurt, melted cheese, or guacamole (without the spices). You'll be amazed how many bits of veggies find their way into your child's mouth.

Try not to worry too much about your child's eating habits. Your job is to understand the principles of child nutrition, serve healthy food, and market it creatively. The rest is up to your child.

⚜

Milk Requirements
for Toddlers

Q *At my son's one-year checkup, the pediatrician said he should have only 16 ounces of cow's milk a day, supplemented by juice diluted with water. Isn't milk good for him?*

A Your pediatrician may have a specific nutritional reason for recommending a juice-and-water mixture for your child. Unlike milk, juice is comprised of nearly 100 percent carbohydrates, so babies tend to drink a lot of it without getting filled. That's why your pediatrician wisely advised you to dilute the juice. Consider juice an extra source of nutrition and fluids but not a replacement for the balanced nutrition of milk. Use 100 percent juice and avoid "junk juices," which contain little juice and a lot of sweeteners.

If your doctor believes that it's necessary to cut down on your baby's daily milk intake, supplement with extra solids and plain water. In general, children between one and two years of age need 24 to 32 ounces of milk per day. Because growing babies need extra fats, use whole milk instead of low-fat until age two, unless your baby is becoming obese or there is a strong family tendency toward obesity. In this case, begin using 2 percent milk around eighteen months.

𝒢

Introducing Cereal

Q *My son was born two months premature and weighed 5 pounds at birth. He's four months old now, and I just increased his formula intake to 6 ounces per feeding. However, he gets hungry every couple of hours. Is it safe to start feeding him cereal?*

A You are learning an important principle of infant feeding: Babies know better than anyone else how much and how often they need to eat in order to thrive. Furthermore, your baby was two months premature. For catch-up growth, premature babies need about 25 percent more formula per day than term babies do.

You can offer solid food between or after formula feedings. Start by placing a fingertipful of mashed banana on your infant's tongue. If it goes in and he approves with a big smile, then he is ready. If it comes right back at you with a disapproving grimace, he's not ready. Wait two weeks before trying again.

Here is a solid-food progression that has worked in the Sears family:

1. mashed, ripe banana
2. rice or barley cereal
3. pureed pears
4. pureed sweet potatoes

5. pureed avocados

When it comes to feeding, don't be afraid to attend to your baby's hunger cues. What, how much, or how often to feed your infant is something you and your baby will work out together as you establish a mutually satisfactory feeding routine.

✑

Food Allergy Signs

Q *I think my baby is allergic to her formula. I tried breastfeeding, but she was gassy and didn't seem to be getting enough milk. So our pediatrician put her on formula. We've tried three different ones, but she now has a constant runny nose and a rash on her cheeks around her mouth. She is also irritable after feeding. What are signs of food allergy?*

A If your baby is particularly fussy after her feedings, she may be allergic to her formula. While you were breastfeeding, she may have become allergic to a food in your diet (dairy is a common culprit).

Symptoms of formula or food allergy include a red, sandpaperlike rash on her cheeks or a red, raised rash around her anus, bloating, diarrhea, and colicky abdominal pain after eating. If you suspect food allergies are at the root of your baby's symptoms, continue to try different formulas. Don't stop looking for answers until this problem is resolved. Talk with your doctor.

&

Foods That Keep Children Awake

Q *My sixteen-month-old son has the most difficult time relaxing to go to sleep. Each night I spend time nursing him before bedtime, then he toddles into the den to say good night to his father. Invariably, he and his dad have what they call "picky parties," where my husband delights in sharing his bedtime snack with junior, including sips of cola or bites of sugary cookies. I'm thinking that Dad's snacks may be keeping our son alert and awake long after his normal bedtime. Or am I to blame for something I've eaten that he gets with the breast milk? Can you list some foods that keep babies up at night?*

A It's no surprise that foods containing caffeine top the list of "sleepless" menus for adults and children alike. Caffeine stimulates the production of adrenal hormones, which induce higher heart and breathing rates and increased urinary output and stomach acid production. Basically, caffeine's effect on the body is the direct opposite of sleep. The degree to which caffeine interferes with sleep varies with the individual; some adults and children are more sensitive to caffeine than others are.

Coffee, colas, and tea are typically high in caffeine, as are many cold and headache remedies (contrary to popular belief, chocolate is not an offender). If you are still breastfeeding, you should know that caffeine can pass through the milk of a breastfeeding mother and thus disrupt her baby's sleep. Caffeine enters breast milk in such small quantities, however, that a nursing mom would have to drink six cups of coffee for it to have a noticeable impact on her baby. Still, the amount that causes problems does vary from person to person. Every breastfeeding mother needs to be aware of how much caffeine she can consume without affecting her baby.

In older babies, watch for sensitivity to cane sugar and artificial colorings, which can interfere with sleep. Some children are more vulnerable to the effects of junk food than others, and this may be what is keeping your toddler wide awake when he should be in dreamland.

☙

Encouraging Toddlers to Eat Their Veggies

Q *My toddler hates vegetables, and I'm worried that she is missing important nutrients. How can I encourage her to eat more healthfully?*

A Many parents share your concern about their toddler's refusal to eat vegetables. A recent study found that the average preschooler doesn't get the recommended five daily servings of fruits and vegetables. In fact, most children in the study ate less than half a serving of vegetables and only two servings of fruits each day.

You can encourage your toddler to eat healthy foods by presenting fruits and vegetables in an attractive kid-pleasing manner. Try these tips from the Sears family kitchen:

• Make a "nibble tray" using a muffin tin or ice cube tray. Fill each compartment with bite-size portions of various fruits and vegetables, then give them catchy names your child will love: broccoli trees, orange wheels, carrot fingers, avocado boats, cantaloupe balls, and so on. Reserve two compartments for nutritious dips, such as guacamole (without the spices), peanut butter, or yogurt. Toddlers love to dip, and allowing them to do so increases the chances that the vegetables will make it into their mouth. Keep the tray on a low shelf of the refrigerator so your child can help herself to nutritious food throughout the day.

- Play the color game at mealtime (and generally, the more color, the more nutritious the meal). Ask your kids, "Have you had your reds (tomato and watermelon), your yellows (papaya, carrots, squash, and cantaloupe), and your greens (broccoli, green beans, and avocado) today?"

- If you really want to have fun with your toddler, don your old overalls and plant a vegetable garden in your backyard. Or grow plants in a flowerpot or bushel basket on the patio if your yard is not conducive to gardening. Toddlers are more likely to eat what they help grow (you can call fruits and vegetables "grow foods"), and they'll also learn something about where food comes from.

- Make veggie art. Create colorful pancake and waffle faces with olive-slice eyes, tomato ears, a mushroom nose, a bell pepper mustache, and many other playful vegetable features.

- Use vegetables as finger foods and dip them in a favorite sauce or dip, such as cheese, yogurt, and avocado dips. Show and tell her how to dip broccoli trees in a melted cheese sauce and call it "cheese on trees."

- Slip grated or diced vegetables into her favorite foods, such as quick breads or muffins.

- Steam the greens. Steamed vegetables are more flavorful and often sweeter than raw or boiled. Sprinkle the steamed vegetables with a favorite cheese, such as Parmesan or cheddar, to boost flavors and add calcium.

- Take your veggie-refuser shopping. The supermarket is

one giant nutritional classroom. As you stroll down the produce aisle, point out how different colors make her grow big and strong, run faster, and be smarter. Each time you go shopping, have her pick out two reds, three greens, and one yellow.

Keep in mind that children should ideally eat three to five servings of veggies a day. For a preschooler, a serving is about 3 tablespoons.

&

Zinc: A Boost to the Immune System

Q *I read about a recent study that said that daily zinc supplements might reduce respiratory infections in preschoolers. The article also said that zinc could help prevent diarrhea and provide protection from illness. Should I give my eighteen-month-old a daily supplement?*

A The study that you are referring to was published in *Pediatrics,* the scientific journal of the American Academy of Pediatrics. Researchers from Johns Hopkins School of

Public Health in Baltimore and the All-India Institute of Medical Science in New Delhi, India, evaluated the effect of zinc supplementation on 298 infants and children aged six months to thirty-five months and compared them with a nonsupplemented group of about the same size. The infants in the supplemented group received a daily dose of 10 milligrams of zinc for six months.

At the end of the study, the supplemented group had higher concentrations of zinc in their blood than did the nonsupplemented group, and they experienced half the number of respiratory infections. The authors concluded that zinc supplementation, at least in the study group, could lower the incidence of acute lower-respiratory infections in preschoolers by as much as 45 percent.

The children enrolled in this study were from a low socioeconomic population of urban India and not well nourished. However, even reasonably nourished suburban American children could probably benefit from zinc supplements. Keep in mind that children under a year get zinc in formula or from breast milk, so they don't need additional zinc. Previous research has shown that zinc also helps mobilize infection-fighting white blood cells by aiding them in releasing antibodies.

To make sure your child is getting enough zinc, feed her zinc-rich food or give her a daily supplement of 10 milligrams. Good food sources of zinc include zinc-fortified cereals (which can contain up to 15 milligrams of zinc per ounce), crab, beef, and beans. Three ounces of crab contain 7 milligrams of zinc; 3 ounces of beef contain 6 milligrams; and ½ cup of beans contains 1.2 to 1.8 milligrams.

Zinc supplements are available in capsules and lozenges. You can entice your toddler to take the supplement by hiding a capsule in a spoonful of yogurt or by sprinkling its contents over cereal. Make sure you don't exceed the recommended daily dose. More is not necessarily better or safer. In some cases excess minerals or vitamins can lead to health problems.

In addition to zinc, try these other immune-boosters:

- *Serve foods rich in antioxidants.* Antioxidants help control free-radical molecules that can attack healthy cells. Antioxidants include vitamin C (found in oranges, grapefruits, mangos, tomatoes, broccoli, spinach, peppers, and kale); vitamin E (found in seeds, nuts, grains, and vegetable oils); and carotenoids, such as beta carotene (found in leafy green vegetables, yellow vegetables, and yellow fruits, including cantaloupe, apricots, peaches, carrots, broccoli, collard greens, spinach, kale, sweet potatoes, and yams).

- *Monitor your child's sugar intake.* Research on adults has shown that eating or drinking 100 grams (3 ounces) or more of sugar—the amount in most cans of soda— during one meal can depress the immune system by reducing the white blood cells' ability to fight germs.

- *Encourage your children to eat a nutritious diet and to exercise.* Diet and exercise will help them avoid the dangers of excess fat. Obesity can lead to a depressed immune system by affecting the white blood cells' ability to multiply and produce antibodies.

- *Protect your child from or help her deal with stressful situations.* Stress taxes the immune system by producing hormones that reduce the number of white blood cells that circulate throughout the body. This is why adults and children often get sick during or after a stressful situation.

- *Continue to plan meals that contain a mix of different-colored foods.* By doing so you can often ensure that your child receives a combination of the food groups, as well as infection-fighting foods. But this isn't ground-breaking advice. Our grandmothers advocated balanced meals as a route to good health long before the sophisticated research methods of today proved them right.

Ⓖ

Guidelines for Feeding a Reflux Baby

Q *At four and a half months, my son has gastro-esophageal reflux (GER) and is a reluctant eater. He finally worked up to eating 30 ounces of formula a day, but sometimes he won't take even that much. I'm concerned that he'll never reach 32 ounces a day, which is where my pediatrician says he should be before starting solids. Why is he so uninterested in eating? Should I wait until he eats more before giving him cereal?*

A Your son is refusing to take large volumes of formula because of his reflux condition. With GER, or reflux, the stomach contents are regurgitated into the esophagus, causing an irritation similar to adult heartburn.

Tiny infants have tummies about the size of their fists, and 6 ounces at each feeding may be too much. Try placing a 6-ounce bottle of formula next to your baby's fist, and you'll understand why.

Most infants require 2 to 2.5 ounces of formula per pound per day. As your pediatrician recommended, formula is certainly more nutritious than rice cereal. But thickened feedings are often more comfortable for babies with reflux.

Here are general guidelines for feeding reflux babies:

- *Feed your baby half as much twice as often.* Your baby is likely to tolerate smaller volumes offered more frequently until the reflux subsides.
- *Keep him upright for 30 minutes after feeding.* This will allow gravity to alleviate the reflux.
- *Begin with rice cereal or mashed bananas.* You can even thicken his feedings by mixing 2 tablespoons of rice cereal with 6 ounces of formula. For reflux babies, thickened feedings tend to stay down better (again, taking advantage of gravity).

✍

Dr. Sears on Dr. Spock

Q *I've always been a big fan of the late Dr. Spock, but the recommendations in his last book against meat and milk have me confused. Should I follow his advice, and if so, how can I make sure my child receives the adequate amount of nutrients?*

A I agree with Dr. Spock that a meatless diet is the healthiest diet for people of all ages, including growing children. Studies show that vegetarians have lower incidences of cardiovascular disease and cancer. They also tend to be leaner and less overweight and generally live longer, healthier lives.

I believe that children under age two should not adhere to a strict vegan diet, though. Yes, children can grow normally on a diet of grains and greens but only with frequent dietary monitoring by a nutritionist experienced in vegan diets.

A strict vegan diet, which excludes all animal foods, dairy, and eggs, tends to be most risky during times in a person's life when there are extra nutritional needs, such as during pregnancy and lactation or childhood and adolescence. Although vegetables are rich in terms of nutrients per calories, children may not eat enough veggies to get the nutrients they need, because their stomachs are too small. As a result, kids on a vegan diet run the risk of not getting enough calories.

A motivated mother can creatively overcome this calorie problem. First, do your homework and find out which vegetarian foods pack the most nutrients. Then, instead of three large meals, encourage your child to graze on small, frequent feedings of nutrient-dense vegan foods, such as nut-butter sandwiches, avocado, nuts, pasta, dried fruits, and fruit smoothies. Growing vegan children also need essential fatty acids, which can be satisfied by a daily tablespoon of flax oil.

Here's another reason for thinking carefully before starting your child on a strict vegan diet: Plant foods contain no vitamin B-12, an essential vitamin for a healthy nervous system. Also, plant foods tend to be lower in calcium and other B vitamins. Even though plant foods do contain some calcium, it can be difficult convincing a child to enjoy kale and collards. You're better off giving your child skim milk, which contains no fat but has all the calcium of whole milk. Children under age two should drink breast milk or whole milk or formula.

I believe the healthiest diet for all ages is a pesco-vegetarian diet. This is a meatless diet that includes fish (especially tuna and salmon, because they are rich in healthy oils), dairy products (yogurt is a good choice), and eggs. Some tasty meatless substitutes that children love include meatless chili, garden burgers, black bean burritos, tofu and spaghetti sauce, tofu cubes in a stir-fry in place of beef or chicken, and veggie pizza.

As always, I suggest you talk to your pediatrician if you are considering a different diet; he or she can offer more insight based on your child's unique dietary needs.

᳄

Handling the Picky
Preschooler

Q *What's the best approach for handling a three-year-old who won't eat at mealtimes and refuses to eat what's being served?*

A Feeding children is a combination of good nutrition and ingenious marketing. Your job as a parent is to prepare nutritious food and serve it creatively. The rest is up to your child.

Here are some tips:

- *Allow grazing on nutritious foods throughout the day.* Three square meals is an adult invention that is more about convenience than human biology. In fact, children who graze have fewer blood-sugar swings and are less likely to become grumpy before meals. Keep a nibble tray in the refrigerator, as described on page 42, and encourage your child to snack from it during the day.
- *Plant a mini-garden.* Teach your child that food is fun by planting a garden together (see page 43). Children enjoy eating food they grow and make themselves, and many morsels end up in their mouths along the way.
- *Aim for a balanced week instead of a balanced meal.* Few children have balanced daily nutrition. Kids nor-

mally binge on favorite foods, but over a week or month their eating generally balances out. If you ease up on the pressure to meet daily nutrition quotas, your youngster will eat more willingly at mealtimes. If she doesn't, set a rule that nibble-tray forays must stop an hour before dinner.

• *Avoid the temptation to resort to junk food just to get her to eat.* Children accustomed to a nutritious diet during their first four years know the connection between what they eat and how they feel (nutritious food makes them feel good, while junk food causes a "yucky tummy"). In fact, youngsters used to eating nutritiously are less likely to overdose on junk food even at a birthday party.

&

Treating Bowel Discomfort

Q *My four-month-old baby makes a terrible gasping sound after each bowel movement. The sound gets worse if we lay her on her back immediately after she is done. She is on medication to relieve her cramping and bowel spasms.*

A   The gasping sounds your baby is making are probably the result of intestinal pain. One cause of this could
be a milk or formula allergy. If you are breastfeeding, your
infant may be intolerant of something in your diet—dairy
products, corn, nuts, or caffeine-containing foods, such as
colas, tea, and coffee. If you are formula feeding, try a less
allergenic preparation. Begin with soy formulas and
progress to the least allergenic formulas (Alimentum,
Nutramigen, and Pregestimil).

When your baby feels gassy and bloated, put her in a
warm bath and massage her abdomen, or lay her on the
floor and pump her legs in a bicycling motion. If she
strains to have a bowel movement, a tiny bullet-size infant
glycerin suppository (available over the counter) may
help. Finally, increasing the amount of water she drinks
will loosen the stools and make it easier for her to pass
them.

Your baby may have gastroesophageal reflux, which
causes stomach acids to be regurgitated into the esophagus
after eating, causing a heartburnlike pain. The strain of
having a bowel movement could trigger reflux, causing
your baby to gasp in pain. Keep her upright (at least at a
45-degree angle) for half an hour after each feeding, and
place her on her tummy after feeding when she is awake
(reflux is often worse when baby lies on her back). Babies
usually outgrow reflux by eight months, when they are
able to sit up after feeding.

ↂ

Colic Means Baby
Is Hurting

Q *My three-month-old baby girl was born ten weeks early. I stopped breastfeeding at seven weeks and have been giving her formula. She began eating a lot (6 to 9 ounces at a feeding) and became constipated. My pediatrician suggested that I stop feeding her so much, but now my baby has colic. Although she has no temperature, she is sleeping more than usual. Today she woke up with a hoarse cry. Is this normal for colicky babies because they scream so much?*

A Here is a trade secret we have learned from almost thirty years of practicing pediatrics: Colic is a five-letter word that means "the doctor doesn't know." In our view, it is too easy to tag a baby as colicky and quickly dismiss the problem. We prefer the phrase "hurting baby" to "colicky baby."

Colic can stem from a variety of causes. Your baby may hurt because she is allergic to the formula. In fact, any time you see a change in behavior or bowel habits following a change in feeding, it's reasonable to suspect that the food and the intestines don't agree with one another. Gastro-esophageal reflux (GER), as mentioned above, is another hidden cause of colicky behavior.

To make feeding less hurtful and more pleasant for

your baby, try changing formulas. Milk-based formulas are most likely the cause of her discomfort because of an allergy to the protein in milk. Try switching to soy-based formula. But before making the switch, take note of your baby's usual symptoms so that you can objectively record any changes. If you notice no improvement after a week on soy formula, try a hypoallergenic formula, such as Alimentum, Nutramigen, or Pregestimil. In these protein-hydrolysate formulas, the potentially allergenic proteins have been predigested, so they're easier on baby's digestive system.

Try smaller, more frequent feedings. Some babies, while not allergic to formula itself, simply can't digest too much at one feeding. But overfeeding is probably not the cause of your baby's constipation. It is more likely to cause diarrhea than constipation. Constipation does, however, sometimes mimic colic, resulting in a misdiagnosis. Give your baby an extra 8 ounces of water each day and experiment with formulas that are less constipating. If she strains to have a bowel movement, insert half of an infant glycerin suppository (available over the counter) into her rectum to make it easier for her to go.

The fact that your baby seems to be sleeping more than usual makes us doubt that a formula allergy or GER is at the root of her discomfort. Babies with intestinal upset usually sleep less and wake up frequently with painful cries. Crying accompanied by more sleeping suggests an emotional reason for your baby's discomfort rather than a dietary or medical one—though babies can hurt so much for medical reasons that they sleep more, simply out of exhaustion from crying. Has there been a recent change in caregivers, sleeping arrangements, or the family's lifestyle? If you have recently returned to work, try carrying her in a sling as much as you can on your days off to see if this settles her crying.

Your baby's excessive crying may be the cause of her hoarseness. But it is unusual even for colicky babies to be hoarse. The fact that your little one is crying herself hoarse is all the more reason to get to the bottom of why she is hurting. Keep working to identify any dietary or caregiver changes until you are able to ease your baby's discomfort. Colicky behavior that continues beyond six months strongly suggests an underlying medical cause, but the good news is that even unexplained colic usually passes by six months.

✍

Overcoming Obesity

Q *My preschooler is very short and extremely overweight. Because he has a hard time running and playing with the children at day care, he gets picked on. But whenever I say no to seconds or dessert, he gets angry. I want to help resolve this health problem, but I don't want him to think I'm saying he is too fat. How can I help my son with his weight problem without destroying his rapidly diminishing self-confidence?*

A If your child is extremely obese, he needs special help. As a caring parent, you need to help your child trim his weight. It is important to realize, however, that the best you can do is create the conditions that motivate him to want to lose weight; the rest is up to him. Here are some suggestions:

- *Get professional help.* If your young child is significantly overweight, talk with your pediatrician about weight-loss counseling. A professional counselor will monitor your growing child's nutrition and develop a workable weight-loss plan. Crash diets are not safe for anyone, especially growing children. Your child needs adequate nutrients for optimal growth while he loses body fat.

- *Try to determine why your child is overweight.* Is it because he eats too much, exercises too little, or a combination of both? Observe his eating habits and special cravings. Does his basic temperament contribute to his obesity? Is he quiet and sedentary or relatively active? Is there a family history of obesity? What body types do you, his dad, and other close relatives have? If your child is physically active and not a couch potato, you can worry less. If he is sedentary or obesity runs in your family, you need to worry more. Besides eating habits, the two most influential factors determining a child's eventual obesity are his inherited body type and temperament. If both parents are obese, a child is at high risk for obesity. If one or both parents has an ecto-morph body type (tall and lean), a child may go through a normal "stretching" period and trim down naturally.

- *Examine your family dynamic about weight.* What is your child's motivation to eat healthfully? Self-motivation is indispensable in any successful healthy eating program. Instead of talking about weight loss, focus on everyone in the family "being healthy."
- *Work out a realistic diet.* In consultation with a professional weight-control manager or nutritionist, teach your child healthy eating habits (we prefer this phrase to "diet"). Help your son distinguish between foods that are healthy and those that are simply fat-producing.
- *Do a nutritional analysis for your child.* Write down everything he eats (food types and amounts) every day for one week. Your nutritionist can then use this information to calculate calorie and nutrient counts and identify those foods he should avoid. A reasonable diet for your child would be 20 to 25 percent fat, 15 to 20 percent protein, and the rest complex carbohydrate. Of the fat, no more than 30 to 40 percent should be saturated fat.
- *Become a label reader.* Unsaturated fats, such as those found in fish and vegetable oils, are good fats. The unhealthiest, and most fat-producing, are synthetic fats found in most packaged foods. Avoid foods with hydrogenated or partially hydrogenated oils in their ingredients as well as junk sugars, such as frostings, icings, and candies. Junk sugar is quickly absorbed in the bloodstream and triggers the insulin cycle, which causes excess fat to be stored in fat cells. Replace junk sugars with plenty of fresh fruits and raw veggies for snacks,

and serve whole-grain breads and cereals for complex carbohydrates.

- *Shape his eating habits.* Change the way meals are served at your house. Your son will probably eat less if the family fills their plates in the kitchen and then takes them to the table (out of sight, out of mind). Use smaller plates, cut foods into smaller pieces, and encourage everyone to eat slowly. Fill up on salads with low-calorie dressing before the main course. Above all, discourage eating when bored, while watching TV, or when the child has nothing else to do.

- *Model healthy exercise habits.* For an extremely obese child, diet alone rarely works. A vigorous exercise program must accompany the diet. You may need to become a walking or bike-riding family in order to help your son. Go to the park and walk the trails together. Climb the jungle gym with him and swim together as a family. Ideally, he should exercise vigorously for at least a half hour a day to burn off approximately ½ pound of fat per week. Motivate your child to persist with his daily exercise program for at least a month, using rewards if necessary. After a month of daily workouts, most children feel so much better that they're motivated to continue.

- *Keep the ultimate goal in mind*—to help your son not only lose fat but also develop a trim body that he is proud of and will continue to maintain. Muscle acts as a natural fat burner; increasing muscle mass naturally burns off fat.

- *Focus on self-esteem.* Identify the skill your son is best at and foster his development in that area. This will

ensure that his sense of self involves more than just his
body image. If your child excels at something that is
important to him, the good feeling is likely to carry over
into other areas and will encourage healthier eating
habits.
* *Be patient.* Reaching his weight goal will be a slow
  process, and your son needs your support every step of
  the way.

   Obesity is a major problem. The earlier in life your son
adopts healthy eating habits, the more likely he will be to
carry these practices into adulthood.

✍

Good Health for
Bottlefed Babies

Q *For medical reasons I will be unable to breastfeed
my baby. What extra precautions can I take to ensure my
baby's health and meet her nutritional needs?*

A Your doctor can help you choose the right formula
to meet your baby's nutritional needs. But there are many
other things you can do to promote your baby's physical
and nutritional health.

- *Eat well during pregnancy.* Nurturing your baby begins in the womb. Take good nutritional care of yourself during your pregnancy to give your unborn baby a healthy start. You'll find useful information about a complete program of nutrition and exercise in *The Pregnancy Book* (Little, Brown, 1997).
- *Stay in touch.* Research shows that touching and interacting with a baby stimulate her physical, emotional, and intellectual health. Hold your infant as much as you can during the first year, providing lots of eye-to-eye and skin-to-skin contact. This physical closeness will enhance your connection with your little one and help your baby get smart from the start.
- *Make feedings special.* Two aspects of the breastfeeding relationship contribute to an infant's sense of well-being: the nutrients in milk itself and the increased holding that breastfed babies get. As well as delivering nutrition, feeding is a social interaction. When bottlefeeding, cuddle your baby as much as you would if you were nursing.
- *Wear your baby in a baby sling as much as possible.* In addition to providing physical contact, the motion of being carried will enhance your little one's growth by providing calming effects.
- *Share sleep.* Sleeping with your baby provides the security of nighttime touch and enhances emotional development. This is especially important for parents who work outside the home. High-touch nighttime parenting will allow you to reconnect with your baby and make up for missed touch time during the day.

Above all, respond to baby's cues in a nurturing way. Ignore any advice to let your baby cry it out. The key word for infant development is "responsiveness." Years ago at an annual meeting of the American Academy of Pediatrics, Dr. Michael Lewis, Professor of Pediatrics at Rutgers University, reported that after reviewing all the scientific studies on what makes babies smarter and healthier, he found the most important factor to be the caregivers' responsiveness to the baby's cues.

The parenting style you choose is crucial to your infant's development, and making yourself available and responding to baby's cues in a nurturing way are vitally important to giving your baby the healthiest start possible.

✥

Calcium Requirements

Q *My healthy three-year-old son refuses to drink milk and doesn't eat cheese or yogurt. I'm concerned about his calcium intake, and I started giving him chewable calcium carbonate (600 milligrams per day) with his breakfast (cereal, no milk). Is that okay?*

A Your three-year-old needs around 500 milligrams of calcium per day, which he gets in the supplement and other foods in his diet. Because most foods contain at least some calcium, it's unusual for American children to be calcium-deficient.

The best sources of calcium for non-milk-drinking children are yogurt and cheese. If your child doesn't like yogurt alone, try making a yogurt smoothie (see pages 7–8). Disguise cheese in other foods, such as scrambled eggs. Green, leafy vegetables are another calcium source, although dairy products provide more concentrated calcium. Canned salmon, in which the bones are mashed, is another rich source of calcium. We suggest that you continue with your calcium supplements until your child begins to eat yogurt or cheese.

☙

A Limited Diet

Q *My three-year-old son eats nothing but crackers, cheese, buttered toast, milk, and apples. It takes several screaming matches to get him to eat even a few spoonfuls of any other food. He cries and complains that it hurts his stomach. Could there be an underlying problem?*

A To prevent a nutritional deficiency, it's important for a child to eat a wide variety of foods, including grains, vegetables, legumes, dairy, meat, seafood, eggs, pasta, and oils. Although your child eats many dairy products, a diet high in dairy may be deficient in iron, a nutrient necessary to make red blood cells for the growing child.

Have your doctor check your child's blood-iron content. This is usually done with a simple finger-stick test. New studies have shown that children with normal hemoglobin may still be iron-deficient. Ask your doctor to do a serum-ferritin blood test, which requires taking several drops of blood from a vein in your child's arm. Iron is vital for a school-age child because iron deficiency (even with normal hemoglobin) can affect intellectual development and school performance in addition to physical growth.

It sounds like you need to do some creative marketing to your selective eater. Here are some tips:

- *Cut down on dairy products and substitute more varied foods.* For finicky eaters, dipping and grazing are two ways to introduce a variety of healthy foods. Create nutritious dips with yogurt, avocados, and peanut butter. Since your son likes cheese, make a cheese dip for dunking broccoli trees and other veggies.
- *Make nutritious concoctions.* Capitalize on your son's fondness for dairy products by adding them to other nutritious foods, such as our fruit-and-yogurt smoothie (see pages 7–8). Our smoothie recipe contains flax oil that provides nutritious fatty acids that are lacking in your child's current diet.
- *Appoint him assistant chef.* Children are more likely to eat what they make, so encourage your son to help you prepare dinner. Or bake homemade breads and muffins together.

- *Plant a garden.* This is a great family activity, and children like to eat vegetables they grow. To introduce vegetables to our reluctant five-year-old, we grew foot-long zucchini (which, incidentally, made great pancakes).

♋

Lack of Concentration and Poor Eating Habits

Q *We are concerned about our preschool daughter's lack of concentration and poor eating habits. She seems to have difficulty focusing on a specific task, whether it's cleaning up her toys or eating a meal with the family. We've tried a reward system and time-outs, with little or no improvement. We've even tried removing her plate and sending her to her room. Also, our daughter eats very little for lunch at school, but at home on the weekends she's as hungry as a bear. We anxiously await your suggestions.*

A To determine whether or not your child is getting adequate nutrition, do a week-long nutritional analysis: Record the type and amount of food your daughter eats at each meal, each day, for a week. Use a nutritional counting book (available in paperback listing the nutritional value of common foods) to add up the number of calories she eats each day and the percentages of protein, carbohydrates, and fats. Besides being educational for you, a nutritional analysis reveals the types and amounts of foods your child lacks.

A preschooler should ingest an average of 40 to 45 calories for each pound of weight. Ideally, your daughter's diet should consist of 15 to 20 percent protein, 60 percent carbohydrates (preferably complex carbohydrates), and 20 to 25 percent fat. Your child is unlikely to achieve a balanced diet every day, so aim instead for a balanced week. If her weekly food count averages these amounts, she is getting enough to eat of the right foods.

Encourage your daughter to graze on nutritious foods, such as fruits, grains, yogurt, and homemade granola cookies, throughout the day. Grazing is a healthy eating habit for busy school-age children.

Do not punish your child over food issues; even time-outs can be punitive. Rewards, likewise, are not appropriate for food issues. Eating must be a completely calm, pressure-free event. You simply supply the food and zip your lip.

To get your daughter to focus more effectively on tasks, sit with her, engage her in conversation, and do the task with her. This approach can even help improve your daughter's focus on eating. A principle I've used as a scout master to keep young cub scouts focused is called KISMIF: Keep it simple, make it fun. A preschooler's attention span tends to be rather short, but your child is more likely to pay attention if a task is fun.

Give your daughter tasks and responsibilities at home

and explain the consequences of shirking an assigned job. For example, if she doesn't put away a toy, she doesn't get to play with it for a while. Make your child's responsibilities enjoyable by assigning her fun jobs around the house and giving her a job title. You might even consider paying her a few dimes for helping out.

Clean Plate Syndrome

Q *My daughter won't give my grandsons, ages three and two and a half, dessert unless they clean their plates. Sometimes she threatens them with taking away their toys as well. Both of my grandsons seem to have good appetites, and they're not picky eaters. I don't think threats lead to good eating habits, do you?*

A Using bribes or threats to get children to eat is a common but unwise practice many adults try. We call this the "clean plate syndrome." Many children don't clean their plates because their parents put too much food on them in the first place. Besides, it is not the parent's job to fill their child's stomachs as much as it is the child's job to develop and exercise his or her own internal appetite controls. And power struggles over food can lead to power struggles elsewhere.

When it comes to portion size, it's far better to dole out small dollops of food and replenish plates when the first helping is gone. Children have tiny tummies, and the concept of three square meals a day is largely an adult invention created more for convenience than for healthy nutrition. The human body, especially a child's body, does better on five mini-meals a day rather than the standard three large ones. Children are naturally grazers. By letting them follow their instincts, parents will reap the benefit of avoiding the midmorning and midafternoon blood-sugar-related mood swings that occur when children aren't allowed to have between-meal snacks. But these snacks must be healthy—no junk food, soda, or cookies, except once in a while for a real treat.

Children by nature have erratic eating habits. They seldom eat from a balanced variety of fresh fruits, vegetables, whole grains, and low-fat meats or fish at every meal, or even every day. Many kids tend to eat a variety of vegetables one day and then refuse to touch them the next day. The point? Strive for a balanced week. Think in terms of what your child eats over a seven-day period, not what he does or doesn't eat one day.

When it comes to withholding dessert, on the other hand, your daughter may be onto something. Parents need to teach their children to first eat the food they need; only after that should they eat the food they want. In our family, we insist that our children eat "grow foods" before they eat "fun foods."

Encourage your daughter not to make food a control

issue but to serve a choice of nutritious foods and market the food creatively. The rest is up to the children.

❧

Organic Foods

Q *My son is two years old, and I'd like to know if you think I should feed him organically grown vegetables instead of those that are sprayed with pesticides. Is it worth the cost, or am I being overly cautious? I'm having trouble finding information on this matter.*

A Organically grown food is always better. Mother Nature makes safe and nutritious fruits and vegetables, and the less interference in its production the better.

The Environmental Protection Agency maintains standards for food producers that include "allowable limits" of certain pesticides in food. These limits are based on experiments in which different amounts of these pesticides are fed to animals that are then monitored for signs of health problems. But how do you test for IQ changes in a lab rat? Not that your child's IQ is necessarily affected by the ingestion of pesticides, but the experts really don't know. Animal testing may prove that these pesticide levels are not overtly harmful to you or your child's health, but the tests cannot prove that they are safe either. Scientists have not tested—and cannot test—for subtle physical and mental effects. We don't know if food with low levels of pesticides is safe for kids. Whenever possible, avoid the risk of giving your child potentially harmful chemicals.

Also, these allowable levels of pesticides are for adult bodies only, not for the smaller, growing bodies of children. A child's metabolism is different from that of an adult, especially in its rapid growth and cell turnover. This makes a child particularly susceptible to the damaging effects of carcinogens on cells undergoing rapid growth, possibly increasing the child's risk of developing cancer later in life.

Raising a healthy child means removing as many health risk factors as possible. Feeding your child organic foods removes an important risk factor and is well worth the extra cost. As more parents demand organic food free of pesticides and hormones, farmers, wholesalers, and grocers will cooperate to provide it. Then you should see the prices come down, and it will become easier for us to feed our children food that will not endanger their development and growth.

◎

A Healthy Breakfast to Fuel Preschoolers

Q *I read that kids who eat breakfast perform better at school. What should I feed my two preschoolers to make sure they get the nutrients that they need?*

A New research is proving what Mom already suspected: Children who eat a nutritious breakfast are better behaved, pay closer attention, participate more in class discussions, and can manage more complex problems than breakfast skippers can. Breakfast sets the nutritional pattern for the rest of the day. If your child misses that first important meal, she is a candidate for erratic bingeing, cravings for junk food, and overeating throughout the day.

A nutritious breakfast should be a balance of complex carbohydrates and proteins. A breakfast composed primarily of only one or the other simply won't do the job. Carbohydrates sedate the brain, and proteins perk it up. But when they're combined, the two help usher amino acids from the proteins into the brain, which sparks learning processes. In other words, complex carbohydrates and proteins act like biochemical partners. This principle is called synergy, meaning that the combination of two nutrients works better than one, sort of like $1 + 1 = 3$.

Research also shows that children who add a high-calcium food to this nutritious breakfast combo, such as yogurt, milk, or cheese, which is high in both protein and calcium, show an even greater enhancement of behavior and learning.

In addition to feeding your kids a healthy breakfast, it's important to send them off to school in a calm mood. Morning chaos or tension increases the levels of stress hormones in the bloodstream, which can affect behavior and learning in two ways:

1. Stress hormones can disturb the brain.
2. Certain stress hormones, such as cortisol, increase simple carbohydrate (such as sugar) cravings throughout the day. Eating too many simple carbohydrates will cause rapid rises in blood sugar, then rapid crashes.

Here are examples of nutritious breakfasts with balanced complex carbohydrates and proteins:

- Granola cereal, yogurt, and sliced apple
- Scrambled eggs, toast, and calcium-fortified orange juice
- Veggie omelet, bran muffin, and fruit with yogurt
- Whole-grain pancakes or waffles topped with berries and/or yogurt, and a glass of milk
- Breakfast "pizza" (basically a large whole-grain pancake filled or topped with fruit or fruit-concentrate-sweetened jelly), plus orange slices or a banana, and a glass of milk
- Whole wheat zucchini pancakes topped with fruit, and a glass of milk
- French toast topped with fruit, and a glass of calcium-fortified orange juice

- Low-fat cheese melted on toast, and a piece of fruit
- Low-fat cream cheese on a whole-grain bagel, and a glass of orange juice

If the breakfast time in your household resembles the hectic morning rush hour in our home, you know that sleepy kids and hurried parents are not a good match for a healthy breakfast. Check out the Sears family rush-hour recipe for a delicious, nutritious smoothie on pages 7–8. We whip these smoothies up when we don't have time to prepare breakfast. (Cut the fruit up the night before to save time.) Not only do we give it to our children, but we also love it ourselves. A great advantage to this smoothie is that you can add almost any supplement your child needs but refuses to take. The addition is unlikely to affect the taste—which makes serving it hassle-free! (*Note:* Kids under two seldom need low-fat products.)

✺

Kids and Artificial Sweeteners

Q *What are the effects, if any, of giving kids drinks or food products that contain NutraSweet? I have a toddler and wonder if it is okay to give him this artificial sweetener.*

A In general we don't recommend giving artificial sweeteners to children. Some scientific studies suggest that artificial sweeteners can promote hyperactivity and impair a child's ability to think and learn, while other studies show no harmful effects. Given the lack of definitive evidence, it makes sense to err on the side of safety. In other words, "When in doubt, leave it out."

The scientific controversy revolves around the quirky biochemical makeup of artificial sweeteners. NutraSweet (aspartame) is composed of two amino acids: aspartic acid and phenylalanine. When sugars from food enter the brain, they are accompanied by amino acids, which occur naturally in foods and in the right balance for easy use by the brain. But when aspartic acid and phenylalanine enter the brain, they come unaccompanied by any such cushioning nutrients. Theoretically, this is where the problem arises. These amino acids bombard the brain and, supposedly, throw its neurotransmitters—and your child's mood and learning abilities—out of kilter.

Common sense indicates that feeding the brain an unnatural substance may cause it to perform in an unnatural way. The best way to curb a yearning for sweets is to ease tartness into your child's diet. That will help his taste buds regain their sensitivity to sweetness, and they will return to being satisfied with less sugar.

Healthy alternatives to both sugar and artificial sweeteners include fruit concentrates and fructose sugar. Fructose sugar is the primary sugar in many fruits and the easiest on the brain. Because fructose is more steadily absorbed and metabolized in the bloodstream, it doesn't produce the same roller-coaster effect on a child's moods as does refined sugar. Fructose is sweeter than table sugar. While the amount of fruit concentrate you should use depends on your own taste, as a general guide, use a third to half as much fruit concentrate as you would sugar in a recipe. For example, if a recipe calls for 2 tablespoons of sugar, use 2 teaspoons to 1 tablespoon of fruit concentrate. Fructose is also available in crystalline form in most supermarkets and all health stores.

Try using high-fructose fruit concentrates, particularly pear and apple, which are available in supermarkets. Fruits like prunes, pears, sweet cherries, peaches, and apples are also excellent sources of fructose. You may want to try the following:

- *Fruit toppings.* Use crushed pineapple, applesauce, berries, cherries, or peaches on your pancakes and waffles. Cooking can increase the level of sweetness in many fruits, which concentrates the carbohydrates. A banana that has been sliced or split lengthwise, and broiled until it bubbles and starts to brown, becomes so intensely sweet it can be used as jam. Apples and pears briefly stewed in very little water until they are tender make wonderful sweet and healthy toppings. Add a dash of vanilla extract and sprinkle on some cinnamon to enhance the fruit's natural sweetness.

- *Honey or maple syrup.* While not as nutritious as fruits, honey and maple syrup contain more fructose than does table sugar. Honey also contains traces of calcium, phosphorus, magnesium, iron, B vitamins, and vitamin C. Maple syrup contains traces of iron and calcium.

- *Cinnamon.* This is a sweet spice, and a small amount goes a long way. It is also nutritious: 1 teaspoon contains 28 milligrams of calcium and traces of B vitamins, fiber, and iron. Use cinnamon sticks as a healthy alternative to sweeten hot drinks, like apple cider or any other juice you drink heated. A sprinkling of cinnamon combined with 1 teaspoon of vanilla extract in a glass of warm or cold milk also makes a delicious sweet drink.

Dr. Keith Conners, author of *Feeding the Brain,* advises that children who are already hyperactive avoid artificial sweeteners. Why take the risk for something that has no nutritional value? Artificial sweeteners contain 4 calories per teaspoon versus sugar's 16 calories. Saving 12 calories isn't worth the doubts about artificial sweeteners.

☙

Preschoolers Who Refuse Dinner

Q *According to his teachers, my three-year-old eats like a horse with all his pals at day care. But he won't eat a thing for dinner once he gets home. Why does this happen and what should I do?*

A It sounds like your child is in the "monkey see, monkey do" phase. If his pals eat a lot, he does, too. But this isn't a problem. Whether at home or at day care, you cannot, and should not, try to control how much your child eats. The quantity your son is eating is far less important than the nutritional quality of the food.

However much your son eats, insist on nutritious meals. Serve him nutrient-dense foods that pack a lot of vitamins and minerals into a small number of calories, such as fruits, vegetables, and grains. Avocados, for example, are especially nutrient-dense. Juice "drinks," containing a little juice and a lot of sweeteners, are nutrient-poor. They contain a lot of calories but very little nutrition. (Ditto this warning for sodas!)

Many children prefer to eat a single big meal and then nibble and snack throughout the rest of the day. Grazing is a very healthy way for children to eat and helps to avoid blood-sugar-related mood and energy swings.

You can encourage grazing by preparing a nibble tray, as described on page 00. When your son gets home, let him graze for the rest of the day. Even if he won't eat anything at dinner, make him sit at the table for a little family time. He might surprise you and start eating when he sees everyone else dig in.

Try to make a surprise visit to the day care center at lunchtime to evaluate the nutritional content of the food served there. Suggest some healthy food choices to your caregiver, and be sure the lunch isn't low in key nutrients. Watch out for foods with a lot of sugar and fat content or artificial coloring. Fatty foods with hydrogenated oils, like potato chips, are particularly bad because they fill kids up and leave less room for the good stuff. Some children are allergic to artificial coloring, which has never been proven safe. There is some evidence that artificial coloring may even be carcinogenic when ingested over long periods of time.

✍

Souring the Sweet Cravings

Q *My preschooler craves sugar. I try to limit her sweets and offer fruit or crackers between meals. Still, I find her hoarding cookies when she gets a chance. I've even seen her take a teaspoon and eat pure sugar out of the sugar bowl. Help!*

A You are right to want to sour your child's sweet tooth. Sugar does promote cravings. The more sugar a child eats, the more she wants to eat.

There is a physiological basis for sugar cravings. A high-sugar meal raises the blood-glucose level, which triggers the outpouring of the hormone insulin. Excess insulin lingers in the child's bloodstream, triggering a craving for more sugar. Here are more ways in which sugar can be harmful:

- *Excess sugar depresses immunity.* Studies have shown that the amount of sugar contained in two 12-ounce sodas can depress the body's immune system.
- *Excess sugar sours behavior and learning.* While studies show that some children's learning and behavior are not affected by sugar, many parents report that their child is sugar-sensitive, and behavior and attention span deteriorate when they eat too much sugar.
- *Excess sugar promotes obesity.* Foods high in sugar stimulate the production of enzymes and encourage the body to store food and fat cells.

With these possible harmful effects of excess "junk" sugar in mind, here's how to curb your child's sugar cravings.

- *Change her sweet tooth into a tart tooth.* Many American desserts are sickeningly sweet. When you bake your next apple pie, use about half the sweetener called for in the recipe.
- *Change from junk sugars to healthy sugars.* Remember: Growing children need a lot of energy—at least 50 percent of their daily nutrition in the form of carbohydrates. Healthy carbs (complex carbohydrates) are what Grandma called starches. They are found in vegetables, whole grains, and fruits. Junk sugars, those that promote cravings and other health problems, are found in candies, sodas, frostings, and packaged treats.
- *Encourage grazing on healthy carbohydrate snacks,* such as yogurt and whole-grain cookies made with fruit concentrate instead of sugar, fruits, and vegetables.

Children who graze on mini-meals throughout the day are better able to curb their sugar cravings than kids who stick to three large meals a day. Unlike the roller-coaster effect of junk sugars, healthy complex carbohydrates enter the bloodstream more slowly and don't trigger the ups and downs of the insulin cycle like junk sugars do.

☙

Meeting the Calcium Needs of Dairy-Allergic Children

Q *My daughter is allergic to dairy products. When she drinks milk she gets severe abdominal cramping and diarrhea. What should I do to make sure she gets enough calcium in her diet?*

A If your child is allergic to dairy products, and it sounds like she is, there are many healthy alternatives to milk. The good news about milk allergies is that most children either outgrow their milk allergy or are able to tolerate small amounts of dairy products frequently but not big gulps at one time. For example, while children may have allergic reactions when they drink several glasses of milk a day, they may be able to tolerate snacking on yogurt or cheese. An 8-ounce serving of yogurt provides 450 milligrams of calcium, one-half of a child's recommended daily need for calcium. Hard cheese, such as Parmesan, contains more calcium than the same volume of milk.

Calcium is best absorbed when taken in smaller amounts more frequently with meals. You may find that your child is more tolerant of dairy products when eating small amounts of yogurt and cheese with a meal. For example, you can boost calcium using dairy foods by grating Parmesan cheese on your child's spaghetti or broccoli.

For the best nondairy sources of calcium, serve your child calcium-fortified orange juice, rhubarb, tofu, salmon, black strap molasses, whole grains, soybean nuts, beans, broccoli, spinach, sesame seeds, almonds, and papaya. Vitamin C improves the absorption of calcium, which is why drinking calcium-fortified orange juice makes good nutritional sense.

✍

The Low-Fat Craze

Q *My sister-in-law has her two-year-old on a very low fat diet. He eats mostly nonfat yogurt, egg whites, fruits, and vegetables. He's very thin for his age but seems healthy. Is this good for him?*

A The low-fat craze that is now a fad among adults is not healthy nutrition for children. Growing infants and toddlers need ample fat in their diets. In fact, without proper fats in the diet, they won't grow optimally—physically or intellectually. As a testimony to the importance of fat in a child's diet, 50 percent of the calories in human milk come from fat. Certainly Mother Nature was wiser than modern low-fat-diet proponents!

Without the fat necessary to satisfy hunger, children often overdose on carbs. If you eat more carbohydrates than the body can burn, the excess carbs will be deposited as fat. A low-fat diet for older children and adults can lead to a lean body only if it's part of an overall healthy diet.

Instead of a low-fat diet for your child, think of good nutrition as a "right-fat diet." The healthiest fats are the omega-3 fatty acids present in fish (primarily salmon and tuna), flax oil, and canola oil. In fact, the fats from fish are often dubbed "smart fats."

Two of the healthiest fats for children can be remembered by the two F's—fish and flax. Coldwater oily fish, especially salmon and tuna, are high in the omega-3 fatty acid DHA, which is vital for brain growth. Brain tissue is primarily fat and makes up about 60 percent of the brain and nerves that run every system of the body. Flax oil is a healthy omega-3 fat that can be added to smoothies (see pages 7–8 for recipe).

Besides needing fat for optimal brain growth, children need healthy fats for energy and healthy vision and skin. Monounsaturated fat, found in olive oil, nuts, and nut butter, is the next category of healthy fat. Unless the child has a familial problem with high cholesterol, egg yolk is one more healthy fat for growing children. Fats from animal sources, such as meat and dairy products, are also healthy but in small amounts.

Unhealthy fats that children don't need are called hydrogenated fats, listed on package labels as partially hydrogenated oils. These fats promote heart disease and create cravings for more of these fats. Go through your pantry and get rid of packaged foods that contain the nutritional bad-fat word "hydrogenated."

Good fats provide energy, build healthy cells throughout the body, form healthier brains, and help food taste delicious, so keep your child on a right-fat diet, not a low-fat diet.

✍

Protecting Children
from Diabetes

Q *Diabetes runs in my family. My father has type 2 diabetes, and my mother got type 1 diabetes as a young child. How can I protect my children from this horrible disease?*

A New insights into diabetes show that some types of diabetes are preventable by taking precautionary measures in early life. For example, research shows us that the risk of both types of diabetes can be reduced by proper diet and exercise. For your family, diabetes seems to be very hereditary, especially since your mother got diabetes early in life. Therefore, a healthy campaign is needed to protect your children.

There are two types of diabetes. Type 1, the type your mother had, is the usual form of diabetes, in which the body doesn't produce enough insulin. Type 2 diabetes is found when the body produces enough (or sometimes too much) insulin, but the cells throughout the body don't use insulin efficiently—a condition called insulin resistance. Normally insulin ushers sugar into the cells, so it can be used for energy. Insulin resistance means that the cells by some biochemical quirk don't let the insulin do an efficient job.

To help your children keep diabetes at bay, serve them

complex carbohydrates, those that do not trigger the insulin cycle as erratically as junk sugars (those found in candies, sodas, and packaged foods). The best complex carbohydrates are lentils, chickpeas, nut butters, whole grains, pasta, soy products, and sweet potatoes. Complex carbohydrates are easier on the sugar-insulin system because they have a low glycemic index (GI), which is a measure of how quickly a carbohydrate is digested and how fast it enters the bloodstream and raises the blood-sugar level to trigger insulin. Foods with a low glycemic index enter the bloodstream slowly and trigger the insulin response less quickly, contributing to a steadier blood-sugar level. On the other hand, foods with a high glycemic index (junk sugars) enter the bloodstream quickly and jolt the insulin response.

In addition to feeding your children the right carbohydrates, increase the amount of healthy proteins in their diet. This includes foods such as yogurt, whole grains, vegetables, soy products, and seafood. Also give them the right fats (seafood and vegetable oils).

Besides providing a diet containing the right sugars, more protein, and the right fats, try to get your children moving. Exercise boosts the efficiency of insulin, helping the cells use the sugar. By boosting the efficiency of insulin, exercise removes sugar from the blood before it can be stored as fat. A leaner person has a lower risk of diabetes.

༄

Banishing the
Breakfast Blahs

Q *I get up early to fix breakfast for my preschooler, but she refuses to eat it. If I force her to eat a few bites of scrambled eggs and drink some milk, she vomits. She claims breakfast makes her have a "funny tummy." What can I fix to give her a good start for the day?*

A Some children do get a queasy tummy in the morning and are not keen on eating a big breakfast. However, sending a child to day care or preschool without breakfast is like driving a car without the right fuel. Consider this bit of breakfast research: Breakfast eaters are likely to be higher achievers in school, pay closer attention, and manage more complex problems than breakfast skippers. Breakfast skippers are likely to do poorly, be more inattentive at school, and show erratic eating patterns throughout the day. They also eat less nutritious foods and are more likely to give in to junk-food cravings. Also, breakfast sets the nutritional pattern for the day. When children skip breakfast, they set themselves up for erratic bingeing and possibly overeating the rest of the day.

The best breakfasts contain complex carbohydrates and proteins. These nutrients act like biochemical partners, helping the neurotransmitters of the brain to work better. Since the ideal nutritious breakfast contains a balance of complex carbohydrates and proteins, you should use the following equation for your child: grains + dairy + fruit = balanced breakfast. For examples of nutritious breakfasts, see pages 72–73.

⚘

A Vitamin Boost for Picky Eaters

Q *Do preschoolers need vitamin supplements if they are picky eaters? If so, what should I look for in a supplement?*

A Most preschool children need vitamin supplements, and especially the picky eaters. Because preschool children typically have erratic eating habits, vitamin supplements are like an insurance policy to make sure your child has the adequate nutrients for optimal growth.

Preschoolers also tend to binge eat. They may like vegetables for one week and not touch them for the next two weeks. A multivitamin/mineral supplement can fill in the nutritional valleys in their erratic eating patterns. In studies, schoolchildren who took a daily multivitamin/mineral supplement did better in school than those who did not.

A nutritionally adequate multivitamin/mineral supplement should have at least 50 percent of the RDA (Recommended Daily Allowance) of the essential vitamins and minerals. But there is one vital nutritional element that is left out of vitamin/mineral supplements, and that is healthy fat. Growing brains and growing bodies need healthy fats, and the healthiest are the omega-3 fatty acids primarily found in seafood and such oils as canola oil and flax oil.

To make sure your children get enough healthy fat in their diet be sure they eat at least three servings a week of coldwater fish, such as salmon and tuna, and three servings (1 tablespoon) a week of oils (primarily canola and flax). If your children do not like seafood, you can get omega-3 fatty-acid supplements in capsules. The best fatty-acid supplement is Neuromins (available at most nutrition stores or by calling 1-888-OK-BRAIN). Give your child one capsule a day.

Once your child is over the picky-eating stage and has a consistent, well-balanced diet, multivitamin/mineral supplements become less necessary. Still, the supplements are a good insurance policy at all ages.

⌖

Homemade vs. Commercial Baby Food

Q *My nine-month-old daughter has been eating stage-two commercial baby foods since she was four months old. Lately I've been trying to make her foods—beef, carrots and brown rice, or noodles and chicken—which are pureed but not as smoothly as in the jar. My daughter just leaves the food on her tongue or gags and doesn't seem to be able to swallow it. Do you think the smooth baby food has spoiled her? Shouldn't she be able to eat pieces of food by now? I'm afraid to keep trying, as I don't want her to choke on anything she can't handle.*

A You are wise to take the time and energy to prepare your own baby food in addition to serving the convenient and smooth commercial baby food. At nine months she is ready for less smoothly pureed foods, so don't give up. Introducing solid foods to your baby exposes her to a variety of foods (in addition to breast milk and formula) and shapes her developing tastes. In fact, the foods that babies begin with become their norm, molding their expectations of how food is supposed to taste. If your baby spends her first year eating primarily jarred or canned foods, she learns that this is what food is supposed to taste like. If, however, she eats primarily freshly prepared foods, she learns that the taste of fresh foods is the norm.

Shaping your daughter's tastes early on for fresh foods can help her establish a lifelong preference for more nutritious eating patterns.

In addition to meeting nutritional needs, progressing to solid foods is a developmental feat. If your baby prefers eating solids with her fingers rather than being spoon-fed, let her do so. It will help her develop her fine-motor skills, and a bit of a mess is part of the feeding game. If she completely shuns lumpy foods, stick with the smoother ones. When preparing homemade baby foods, experiment with consistency until you find the one that gets the most food down with the least amount of protest. Choose nutritious foods and present them creatively. Pureed avocados are an excellent source of nutrition at this age.

ℐↈ

Lactose Intolerance

Q *My eleven-month-old daughter has temporary lactose intolerance. How long will this last? I've been feeding her lactose-free formula, but she doesn't like soy. I'm not sure what to feed her when it's time to switch her to regular milk. Also, is it okay to feed her yogurt and cottage cheese?*

A Many infants outgrow their lactose intolerance by two years of age, but the condition may recur later in childhood or adulthood. Continue feeding your daughter a lactose-free formula for three to six more months and then gradually introduce cow's milk as a beverage.

In the meantime, introduce increasing amounts of yogurt. Many lactose-intolerant people can eat yogurt because the lactose in it is adequately processed. Yogurt is a healthy milk substitute and actually contains more calcium than milk.

Keep a diary of your baby's reactions to lactose. Make a chart with three columns. Note the symptoms—for example, bloating, abdominal pain, and diarrhea—in the first column. In the next column, chart the type and amount of dairy products she has eaten. Use the third column to record her reactions. This chart will help you determine the type and amount of dairy products your infant can comfortably ingest.

Juice Abuse

Q *Can a preschooler drink too much juice? My three-year-old lives on apple juice. She drinks several cups a day. Lately, she is drinking more juice and eating less. I'm*

*afraid of a vitamin deficiency. What should I do to elimi-
nate the juice habit?*

A Children enjoy juice, but, as you suspect, too much
of it is not healthy. It can cause your child to be under-
nourished to the point where it can interfere with growth.
Here's why:

- Fruit juice is not a source of balanced nutrition. Most
  fruit juices contain nearly as many calories per ounce as
  low-fat milk, but nearly all the calories in juice come
  from carbohydrates. Children who drink too much juice
  consume calories that take the place of more nutrient-
  dense foods, such as those containing proteins, minerals,
  and healthy fats. Studies have shown that the more juice
  children drink, the less milk they consume.
- The high fructose and sorbitol content of some juices
  (such as pear and apple) can lead to chronic diarrhea and
  diminished absorption of vital nutrients.
- Excessive juice consumption is a subtle cause of obesity,
  since children can overdose on juice and consume many
  fewer nutritious calories.

To encourage less juice and more nutrient-dense foods,
limit your child's juice consumption to less than 12 ounces
a day. Use juice simply to flavor water (one-quarter juice
to three-quarters water). Offer your child water instead of
juice when she is thirsty, and get in the habit of letting your
child see you enjoy glasses of plain water. Since children
have a natural sweet tooth, they will prefer juice to water
unless you model otherwise. Provide 100 percent juice.

Avoid juice drinks, punches, and juice cocktails, which have a lot of added corn syrup and artificial sweeteners.

Encourage her to drink vegetable juices. Vegetable juices are more nutrient-dense than fruit juices, since they pack a lot more nutrition into every ounce. Carrot and tomato juice are two nutritious alternatives to fruit juice. If your child insists on drinking a lot of juice, make your own. Buy a juicer or blender and let your child help prepare the juice. Homemade juice is much healthier since it contains much of the healthy nutrients, pulp, and fiber that are lost in commercial juicing. Of course, eating the raw fruit is much more nutritious than drinking the juice.

✑

Trimming the Family Fat

Q *My husband's family is very obese, and our family reunions are usually all-out fatty-food feasts. What can I do to protect my three young children from following in their relatives' footsteps, craving high-fat, high-calorie foods?*

A You are right to be concerned. You owe it to your children to keep them from being obese. The risk of just about every serious or chronic disease increases proportionally to the amount of extra fat a person has to lug around. It's a fact that lean people are healthier and live longer.

Heredity is one of the strongest determinants of eventual obesity. If one parent is obese, there is a 40 percent chance that the child will later become obese. If both parents are obese, the risk may be as high as 80 percent. In fact, many nutritionists feel that genes are actually a more powerful determinant of obesity than diet.

Obesity affects one in four children in the United States. A recent study showed that there's a 30 percent increase in childhood obesity over the previous decade. This is thought to be due primarily to diet and lifestyle changes: Children today eat more fast foods and exercise less.

But there is hope! Use these suggestions to help your children overcome their inherited fate by implementing a fat-trimming regimen for your family:

- *Raise active kids.* If your children are not active by nature, and especially if they do not have genetically lean body types (if they are more like an apple or pear than a banana), then get them moving more. Plan a family workout. Take walks together, or work out together around the home or at the park. Limit TV watching and increase exercise and outdoor games. If your children like to watch TV, encourage them to work out while they watch. Perhaps you can put a mini-trampoline in your family's TV room. Make your family times active ones, engaging in such activities as hiking in nearby parks or swimming at the local Y.
- *Monitor snacks.* Encourage your children to snack on

low-fat, nutrient-dense foods rather than those that pack a lot of calories but little nutrition.

- *Discourage boredom eating.* Avoid letting your children eat in front of the television set or raid the refrigerator when there is nothing else to do.

- *Supervise their eating habits.* Provide only healthy, nutritional choices. Children left alone while eating will often overdose on junk food. In fact, most family obesity is a shopping problem. If you don't buy and stock junk food in the house, it's not available for children.

- *Model good eating habits.* As you eat, so does your child. If you choose only nutritious foods, your children get the message that this is the normal way of eating.

- *Serve nutrient-dense foods.* Foods that pack a lot of nutrition into a small number of calories include fresh fruits, whole grains, nonfat yogurt, lean meat, fish, veggies, and soy foods. Foods that are nutrient-poor (those that pack a lot of calories into a small amount of nutrition) include soft drinks, fast foods, packaged candies and cookies, most packaged chips and snack foods, marshmallows, and doughnuts.

- *Fill them up with fiber.* Feeding your children fiber-rich foods gives them a feeling of fullness without a lot of calories. Studies show that people who eat a high-fiber diet consume fewer calories per day. As a general guide, a child's age plus 5 grams is the minimum amount of daily fiber a child should get. So, a three-year-old should get at least 8 grams of fiber a day; a five-year-old should get at least 10 grams of fiber daily. Fiber-rich foods include whole-grain cereals (especially bran), flax meal, apples with skin, prunes, kidney beans, lentils, apricots, blueberries, figs, whole-grain bread, barley, spinach, broccoli, pears, sweet potatoes, grapefruit, and whole wheat spaghetti.

- *Avoid hydrogenated fats.* These are factory-made fats that are added to many packaged goods. Besides giving the food a longer shelf life, they add a pleasant feeling in the mouth that makes children want to overdose on the fat-rich food. If you see "partially hydrogenated oil" on the package label, leave the product on the shelf in the supermarket.

- *Avoid the clean plate syndrome.* Let your child leave food on his plate. Remember: Tiny children have tiny tummies—about the size of their fist. Better to dole out small portions and refill the plate if necessary.

- *Frequent restaurants that have salad bars.* Avoid fast-food outlets. Becoming a salad-eating family is one of the best obesity-preventing habits you can adopt to shape your children's growing tastes.

❧

Suggestions for a Sandwich Strike

Q *Do you have any suggestions for a child who refuses to eat a sandwich for lunch? My preschooler stays at day care, and each day we pack her lunch together. I always*

include fruit, fresh vegetable sticks, and a cheese or
peanut butter sandwich. Each day she eats the fruit and
vegetables but returns home with the sandwich untouched.
She cannot be getting enough protein this way. Any sug-
gestions?

A Your concern reminds me of the child who com-
plained to his mother that the sandwiches she made were
too healthy, because none of his classmates would trade
with him. Still, you are correct in encouraging your child
to eat a sandwich. Actually, a peanut butter sandwich on
whole-grain bread is power-packed with protein.

You should teach your daughter how to make her own
sandwich. Children are more likely to eat what they create.
Insist on whole-grain bread, so you can shape your child's
tastes toward whole grains rather than the less nutritious
white bread. You're also right to stress a high-protein
lunch, since proteins tend to perk up the brain, while high-
carbohydrate lunches tend to put children to sleep. With a
high-sugar lunch, children become lethargic and learn less.
A high-fat meal also causes children to be lethargic. It's
also best to skip desserts at lunch and serve them after the
evening meal.

Keep in mind the basic principle of feeding toddlers:
wise nutrition and creative marketing. Sometimes the way
you present a sandwich gives it a fighting chance to get
into the mouth of the child. Using a cookie cutter, cut the
sandwich into fun shapes. Use a bit of veggie art (see
pages 7–11) on the sandwich. Try removing the crust. For
some unexplained reason, some children just don't like
bread crust. And, despite what Grandmother taught, the
crust has no more nutritional value than the rest of the
slice. Oh, and it does not make your hair curly!

If your child still doesn't like sandwiches, pack some high-protein alternatives: fruit-flavored yogurt, a hard-boiled egg, homemade whole-grain cookies, packaged cheese sticks, and milk. Continue to include fruits and vegetables. Send her off to school with a nutritious breakfast (see pages 72–73), follow up with a healthy midafternoon snack, and then serve a nutritious family dinner.

✇

Living with
Childhood Diabetes

Q *My three-year-old was just diagnosed with type 1 diabetes. We're handling it fine, and luckily she is a trooper with the new diet and medication regime. But what about birthday parties? How do I handle snacks at preschool for her? I don't want her to grow up feeling like an odd person. Do you have any healthy and safe ideas?*

A You'll be surprised how well young children handle chronic diseases. In fact, the younger a child is when she gets a lifelong disease, the better she handles it, because it becomes her norm.

The key to helping your child manage her diabetes is to

help her "live" with her difference. You certainly want to encourage her to attend birthday parties, and her eating will become her best teacher. Soon she will learn what foods and what eating habits cause her to feel "yucky." For example, she'll probably get by eating one small piece of cake but will feel terrible if she eats two. Eventually she'll have her own "feel good" and "feel bad" foods list.

An important factor in coping with diabetes is to learn the principle of feeding your child foods with a low glycemic index (GI). The glycemic index is a measure of how quickly a carbohydrate is digested, enters the bloodstream, raises the blood-sugar level, and triggers insulin release. Foods with a low glycemic index enter the bloodstream slowly and trigger the insulin response less quickly, contributing to a steadier blood-sugar level and, consequently, a steadier mood. Foods with a high glycemic index enter the bloodstream quickly. In a diabetic who is low in insulin, this can lead to high blood sugar and out-of-control diabetes.

As part of your child's diabetic teaching, her instructor will give her a list of foods with a low glycemic index, such as whole grains, soy foods, kidney beans, dairy products, apples, chickpeas, spaghetti, sweet potatoes, and most vegetables. You can encourage whole grains and fiber-rich fruits and vegetables. Fiber slows down the absorption of carbohydrates and steadies the blood sugar. Because fruit contains more fiber than juice, it's wise for diabetics to eat whole fruits (apples and oranges) rather than juices, unless they need the juice to pull them out of a bout of low blood sugar.

Teach your child the A's and B's of fiber: apples, artichokes, apricots, and avocados; bran, beans, and berries.

Children with diabetes should graze, snacking frequently on smaller meals throughout the day rather than eating three large meals. In this way, their blood-sugar control is much easier.

In a nutshell, children with diabetes need to eat like everyone else should eat. While nondiabetics can get by with erratic, unhealthy eating habits for a period of time, diabetics cannot. As your child gets older, impress upon her that because of her diabetes she must have different eating habits but that being different doesn't equate with being less.

It's okay for your child to have a small scoop of ice cream at birthday parties, since the fat in the ice cream slows down the entry of sugar into the bloodstream. But regarding snacks at school or a friend's home, it's best to brown-bag it. Healthy snacks for a preschooler with diabetes include yogurt, veggies, fruit, and homemade whole-grain, high-fiber cookies.

ℒℱ

Protein Requirements

Q *I know my eighteen-month-old must be protein-deficient. She hates all meats, poultry, and even cheeses. She still breastfeeds, although she has backed off consid-*

erably. What are some protein substitutes that I can use to "trick" her into getting adequate protein? How much protein does she really need at this age?

A You may be surprised that most American toddlers are rarely protein-deficient. And you may be amazed at how little protein children actually need to grow adequately. From one to six years of age the average child needs only 0.6 grams of protein per pound. About 20 percent of a toddler's total daily calories should be in the form of protein.

Still, you are right to be paying attention, since adequate protein is necessary during the rapid growth stage of toddlerhood. If your toddler needs 15 to 18 grams of protein a day, she can get this amount from any *one* of the following combinations:

- 1 cup of yogurt and 1 cup of cereal
- Tuna fish sandwich (2 ounces of tuna)
- ½ cup of cottage cheese and 1 piece of whole wheat toast
- 2 scrambled eggs with cheese
- 2-ounce hamburger on a whole wheat bun
- 1 peanut butter sandwich (using 2 slices of whole wheat bread and 2 tablespoons of peanut butter) and ½ cup of milk
- 2 8-ounce glasses of milk

While all proteins contribute to growth, some proteins are more powerful growth-promoters than others. Proteins are given a biological value (BV), a rating of how well the body utilizes proteins for growth. Here are the proteins that are highest in biological value:

- Whey proteins (the predominant protein in human milk)
- Egg whites
- Fish
- Dairy products
- Beef
- Soy
- Legumes (beans, lentils)

৶

Worries About a Chubby Baby

Q *I'm concerned because my ten-month-old son is very chubby. He is bottlefed and drinks about six bottles of formula (about 40 to 48 ounces) a day. My pediatrician keeps saying he will slim down as he walks and becomes active. Should I put him on a diet or give him skim milk?*

A As your pediatrician has reassured you, most chubby infants trim much of their baby fat sometime around one year, once they start walking and running. Also, toddlers don't eat as much per pound of weight during the second year as they did the first year. They don't grow as rapidly in the second year as they did in the first, and most toddlers are often too active to remember to eat.

As a general guide for formula requirements, a ten-month-old infant needs about 2 ounces per pound per day. Since six 8-ounce bottles of formula a day is a bit on the high side for this age, you may consider diluting or omitting one of those bottles. You can give your toddler more water, less formula, and more solids, such as vegetables and whole-grain cereal. Don't completely replace the formula with food, since food packs almost as many calories, with less nutrition. Rather than put him on a "diet," emphasize nutrient-dense foods (those that pack a lot of nutrition into a small number of calories, such as formula, yogurt, vegetables, and grains) instead of fruit and juice—foods that are high in calories but don't pack as much nutrition. The Committee on Nutrition of the American Academy of Pediatrics recommends that children under two years of age not be given low-fat milk because infants and toddlers need the extra fat during this rapid-growth stage.

✑

Biting the Breast That Feeds Him

Q *I have nursed my year-old son since he was born. Lately, he's been totally uninterested in nursing. He has front teeth, and all he wants to do is "test" his biting power on me. Well, it hurts! I get so upset and want to wean him, but then I think of all the benefits he's getting. I hate to have these feelings. Anything I can do to chill and help him get ample nutrition and calories?*

A Picture yourself comfortably nestled in a rocking chair nursing your toddler. As you begin to nod off into the sea of tranquillity due to the release of relaxing hormones during nursing, suddenly you are jarred awake by jaws with newly erupted pearly whites clamping down on your sensitive nipple.

As you are finding out from this common yet annoying nursing quirk, babies do bite the breast that feeds them. Remember, your baby does not bite to purposely hurt you. He's using you as a human teething ring because he associates the breast not only with food but also with comfort for those sore little gums.

Naturally you want to wean him when it hurts, but here are some ways to teach your infant nursing manners. These tips can help to protect your nipples during these attacks of sore gums, so you can continue to comfortably nurse your toddler.

- As soon as you feel him begin to chomp, insert your finger between his gums and your nipple. Use your index finger to pull down on your baby's lower jaw to remind him to respect the breast that feeds him.
- Keep your index finger in the corner of his mouth ready to break the suction once he begins to clamp down.
- If your baby does clamp down and won't let go, don't yank your nipple out of baby's mouth, traumatizing your nipple even more. Instead, work your index finger between baby's gums and pry the jaws apart. Then hook the end of your finger around the nipple to protect it as you withdraw it from baby's mouth. Let your finger take the pressure of the biting rather than your tender breast tissue.
- Don't overreact, as it may frighten your baby. While your natural inclination is to quickly pull him off your breast and scream "*No!*," some babies are so bothered by this unexpected reaction that they actually stop nursing for a couple of days. Once he bites, immediately disengage his little jaws from the breast, put him down, and walk away. Soon he will associate biting Mommy with the end of the feeding.
- Tell him it "hurts Mama." This helps teach your toddler to respect your breasts. Once your baby learns to associate an undesirable response to the biting, he will learn to nurse comfortably without biting you.
- Pull him toward your breast. Instead of the yank-yell response, here's a trick that Martha used to successfully

nurse many of our babies through the biting stage. As soon as you sense biting is about to begin, pull him closer into your breast instead of pulling him away. In order to breathe, he will need to open his mouth more and uncover his nose. This unlocks the bite immediately.

• Give him a cold teether to suck on. Biting often occurs during the end of nursing, when baby is filled with milk and wants to suck a while longer for comfort and to relieve sore gums. Once you sense that he's had enough to eat, remove him from your breast and let him continue sucking on a cold teether, such as a frozen banana, cold washcloth, or your finger. Also, you can cool your index finger with cold water and firmly massage his gums with the tip of your finger before feeding.

Biting while nursing is a temporary stage that is most common between six and fifteen months, when those front teeth are erupting. Still, nursing should be pleasurable (otherwise the human race would not have survived). Use the above techniques to get you and your baby through this annoying stage of biting, so you can both settle down to a long-term nursing relationship.

✍

The Health Benefits of Peanut Butter

Q *My two-year-old craves peanut butter. I could give him peanut butter sandwiches, peanut butter dip, or peanut butter spread on bananas every meal, and he'd be perfectly happy. Is peanut butter healthy? I read that it has hardly any saturated fat, so I guess it's okay.*

A Peanut butter is actually one of the healthiest toddler foods because it's so nutrient-dense, meaning it packs a lot of nutrition into a small number of calories. Besides being nutritious, it's convenient. Spreading peanut butter on whole wheat bread or some fruit, such as bananas, is a very nutritious and satisfying meal.

Consider all the nutrients that are in 2 tablespoons of peanut butter, the average amount spread on a peanut butter and jelly sandwich:

- 8.5 grams of protein
- 4 milligrams of the B vitamin niacin (nearly half of the recommended daily amount for a toddler)
- calcium
- folic acid
- zinc
- iron
- fiber

In addition, your toddler gets more than 200 calories (around 15 percent of the daily needs of a busy toddler) in a small peanut butter and jelly sandwich. Even the fat in peanut butter (peanut oil) is comprised of 80 percent healthy unsaturated fats.

Although we praise peanut butter as one of the top toddler foods, especially for picky eaters, here is a checklist to make sure your child's peanut butter experience is a healthy and safe one:

- ☐ Check the label, as brands differ. Avoid peanut butters that contain hydrogenated or partially hydrogenated oils, which increase the shelf life and prevent the oil from separating. Look for these terms on the label.
- ☐ Check to see if the oil separates. You can tell whether or not peanut butter contains hydrogenated oil by checking to see if the oil is separated when it sits on the shelf. When nonhydrogenated peanut butter sits, the natural oil rises to the top, so you have to stir the oil into the peanut butter after you open it. If there is no oil floating on the top of the peanut butter, it probably contains hydrogenated oils. These hydrogenated oils give food such as peanut butter a pleasant taste that children enjoy, but they are unhealthy for a growing child. Since one of your goals is to shape your child's taste toward nutritious foods, you don't want him to develop the "mouth taste" of hydrogenated oils in processed foods.
- ☐ Check to see if your child is allergic to peanut butter. Peanuts are one of the most common and serious food allergens, and children seldom outgrow an allergy to peanuts. If your child is allergic to peanut butter, be sure

to warn the preschool teacher and other caregivers at day care or homes that your child may visit. For more on peanut allergies, see pages 111–13.

☐ Avoid letting your child eat a glob of peanut butter, because this can cause choking. Also check the size of the serving. It's better to spread nut butters on bread or crackers.

Store the unopened jar of peanut butter upside down to allow the oil to settle to the top. This makes mixing it in easier once it's opened.

⃝

Dealing with Dinnertime Disasters

Q *My eighteen-month-old twins have turned mealtime into "dinnertime disaster." There is always someone crying, throwing food, or refusing to eat. My husband gets so distraught, he takes his plate into the den and eats alone. So there I am with two babies to feed, and I end up crying. What can I do to calm down the "wild animals" at my table?*

A   To change dinnertime disasters into a pleasant mealtime requires some food discipline for your busy toddlers.
Try these Sears strategies:

- Get them their own toddler-size table and chairs that
  you call the "special table." (In feeding toddlers and
  getting toddlers to behave, you will get a lot of mileage
  out of the term "special.") If those busy little feet are
  planted firmly on the floor while they are sitting in their
  own child-size chairs, you are likely to keep your toddlers' attention longer.
- Serve small, toddler-size dollops of food on small plates,
  realizing that tiny children have tiny tummies. Too much
  food on a toddler's dish leads to two-fisted eating and
  major mess-making.
- To discourage food flinging and to give the meal a
  fighting chance to make it into your toddlers' mouths,
  put a few small pieces of favorite foods on their plates
  and refill as needed. We have found that spaghetti holds
  a toddler's mealtime attention longer than most foods,
  but put only a few strands at a time on their plates.
- Use toddler plates with suction cups that anchor to the
  table and sippy cups that cannot spill. Or try a trainer cup
  that has two easy-to-grasp handles, a tight lid with a
  small spout, and a weighted bottom on a wide base.
- Fill the cup half full to minimize messes.

Above all, hang in, as this, too, shall pass. Once your
toddlers become more verbal and are able to understand
food instructions (usually around age two), you will find
that these dinnertime disasters are merely a stage from
their messy pasts.

GƆ

Taking Peanut Allergies Seriously

Q *Can you tell me more about peanut allergies? My three-year-old had a severe reaction to peanut butter when she was one year old, and we ended up in the emergency room. The doctor used epinephrine to decrease the swelling so she could breathe. I am afraid of letting her out of my sight now for fear she will eat something with peanuts in it. Would allergy shots help?*

A An allergy to peanuts is one of the most serious food allergies. Not only do the reactions tend to be severe (ranging from a rash to breathing problems, severe wheezing, and anaphylactic shock), but it's also one of the few allergies that children rarely outgrow. Because of the seriousness of this allergy, it is wise to take precautions.

You need to teach your child to watch for hidden peanuts. At age three she can certainly understand not to eat peanut butter. But you need to teach her to look for peanuts hidden in other places, such as candy bars, cookies, snacks, and some Asian dishes. Even a residue of peanut oil in a frying pan can cause a reaction in someone who is highly allergic.

Be sure to warn the school and her playmates' parents about this serious allergy, as your child may neglect to tell them about it when she snacks away from home. Get a safety bracelet for her to wear that alerts everyone else to her peanut allergy. Take along an epinephrine-filled syringe (EpiPen) if you're going camping or somewhere else far from medical services. If your child eats an unknown food that you fear may contain peanuts, take immediate precautionary measures. Calmly drive your child to the nearest emergency room. Sit in the waiting room for an hour. If no reaction occurs, you can safely leave. If there is a reaction, you'll have immediate access to medical care.

A series of allergy shots to build up an immunity is usually not effective against food allergies. However, a new form of allergy shot is on the horizon that may help. Check with your allergist to see when it may be available.

Because of the severity of this allergy, it's natural for you to want to be a protective parent and hover over her. However, the older your child gets, the more she needs to take responsibility for her own allergies, and she will require less surveillance from you.

Peanuts are actually legumes, not nuts, so many people who are allergic to peanut butter can safely eat other nut butters, such as almond or cashew. Try these alternative nut butters, but slowly introduce them in increasing doses. Almond butter is a healthy alternative to peanut butter because it contains half the amount of saturated fat and eight times as much calcium. Cashew butter is less nutritious than almond butter and peanut butter because it contains less protein, fiber, and niacin, but it's still tasty. Another healthy alternative is soy butter. (A word of caution on soy: Soy beans are also from the legume family, so be careful introducing them in case your child is allergic to soy beans, too.)

Finally, it sounds like your child is highly allergic to peanuts, so even a whiff of the peanut allergen could upset her. Take peanut allergies very seriously until your child is old enough to do so herself.

Too Busy to Eat

Q *My two-year-old son is at the low end of the chart in weight and the high end in height. You can imagine how I feel when people ask me if I ever feed him! To be honest, he's too busy to eat. While he will taste almost anything, he gets distracted easily and wants to roam the house rather than sit and finish his meal. I've resorted to putting his food on the coffee table so he can snack as he pleases. Is there anything else I can do to beef him up?*

A Children who are tall on the growth chart are usually low in weight. Often this is because of their inherited body type and usually does not reflect inadequate nutrition.

However, an important principle of nutrition is getting children to eat right for their body type. There are three body types, which we refer to by the names of fruits:

- Bananas—tall and lean
- Apples—medium or stocky
- Pears—short and round

These three types burn calories and store fat in different ways. Bananas are calorie burners, so they can eat and eat and still stay slim. Apples and pears, on the other hand, are calorie storers. Unlike bananas, the rounder people are likely to put on excess weight if they overeat. Obviously apples and pears envy bananas. Sounds like your child is blessed with a banana body type in addition to a busy personality—two traits that are likely to keep him slim. No matter what you feed him, you are unlikely to "beef him up." Genetically lean children (bananas) are likely to look lean no matter how much they eat. Also, busy toddlers are difficult to keep still in any situation, let alone when trying to get them to eat.

Use the toddler nibble tray (page 42), but insist that he sit when he eats. Discourage roaming around the house while eating. Not only is this messy, but it sets up a condition of eating while on the run. This can cause him to get excited and possibly choke on food. If he does like to nibble while roaming, be sure you give him "melt in the mouth" foods.

Here are some safe sit-still strategies. Get him his own child-size table and chair, so his feet can touch the floor. When he eats at the family table, place a small stool under his feet. One of the reasons children don't like to sit still at the dinner table is that their feet dangle, and dangling feet like to get up and run. Be sure to concentrate on nutrient-dense foods, those foods that pack a lot of nutrition into a small number of calories, such as avocados, eggs, fish, kidney beans, lentils, sweet potatoes, tofu, tomatoes, whole grains, yogurt, and flax oil. Also, give your child a multivitamin/mineral supplement as an insurance policy during these picky-eater growing years.

⚘

Perfectionist Preschoolers

Q *My preschooler is a perfectionist in every way. When I put her plate on the table, she spends twenty minutes arranging the food so it looks pretty. I find this very odd behavior and am concerned. She has no problems developmentally, and she is very healthy. She just wants to line up her peas or corn and arrange her fruits so they look pretty. Once they are arranged, she eats everything. Is this odd? What should I do?*

A You have put your finger on an annoying quirk of early childhood—the desire for order. Children normally go through a stage where they become fixated on patterns to the point where if a pattern is not exactly conformed to, they fall apart. The sandwich must be cut on the diagonal, and the alternative is unacceptable. Children will often drink their milk only from their "red cup" and shun any plate that is not their favorite. This odd and sometimes annoying behavior is a passing developmental quirk. As long as she eats her "pretty peas," laugh about her arrangements, and be happy she eats them.

◈

Decreasing Allergy Risks

Q *I come from a highly allergic family. My parents and siblings all have allergies, sinusitis, and mild asthma, and I have eczema. What can I do to protect my six-month-old from horrible allergies? I am breastfeeding her, but I'm nervous about starting solid food. Suggestions?*

A If one parent has allergies, the child's risk of inheriting these allergies may double. The good news is that by taking the following allergy-prevention measures you can lower your child's chances of inheriting your allergies by as much as 50 percent:

1. *Prevent allergies before baby is born.* You can reduce the chances of your child being allergic to the

foods that you are allergic to by limiting your intake of those foods, especially dairy products, during your pregnancy.

2. *Breastfeed your baby as long as you can.* Actually, you are already giving your child the most important allergy-preventive medicine you can by breastfeeding her. The longer you breastfeed, the less chance your child has of developing skin and respiratory allergies. The reason for this is that breast milk is rich in immunoglobulin A (IgA). This antibody coats the intestines like a protective paint and keeps food allergies out of the bloodstream. Formula, especially if your child is allergic to it, can inflame the sensitive intestinal lining. In doing so, it allows potentially allergenic proteins from food to seep through into the bloodstream and sensitize your child to allergies later. Also, until your child is at least one year of age, keep the most allergenic foods out of your diet while breastfeeding. These include dairy products, nuts, egg whites, shellfish, berries, corn, tomatoes, and soy.

3. *Delay the introduction of solid foods.* During the first six months, the lining of your baby's intestines is immature, and it's easier for food allergens to seep into the bloodstream, causing your baby to build up antibodies to those allergens and later become allergic to those foods. Wait until at least seven months before you start her on solid foods, and when you do introduce solids, start with the least allergenic foods first, such as rice, barley cereal, carrots, squash, sweet potatoes, pears, and avocados. Wait until at least eighteen months to introduce highly allergenic foods, such as egg whites, shellfish, peanut butter, tomatoes, and citrus fruits. It's especially important not to

introduce dairy products until your baby is at least one year old.

4. *Feed your child a wide variety of foods.* Children like to binge on several foods at a time. Eating too much of a potential allergenic food can stimulate an allergy to that food. Rotate your child's diet so that she eats smaller amounts of a variety of foods.

5. *Opt for fresh foods.* During the first couple of years give your child as many fresh and additive-free foods as possible. You can easily make your own baby food. The fewer cans and packages you open, the less chance your child has of being exposed to food allergens. Especially avoid food coloring, such as yellow, red, and blue dyes.

For most children, food sensitivities are dose-related. A lactose-intolerant child may eventually be able to drink half a glass of milk with no symptoms. But when she drinks two glasses of milk, she may get abdominal pains. Most children outgrow food allergies by age three. For example, many tomato-allergic toddlers can later safely indulge in ketchup.

🙾

Protein Powder
for Toddlers

Q *Is protein powder safe for toddlers? My sister-in-law uses it in smoothies for her three young children, and they seem healthy. If it's safe, how much should I add to each cup, and what is the benefit?*

A Yes, protein powder is safe for toddlers, and it sounds like your sister-in-law is nutritionally wise. Because most commercial protein powders are soy based, be sure your child is not allergic to soy. Look for signs of food allergies, such as dry, scaly patches of skin on your child's face, bloating, diarrhea, or wheezing. You also have to be careful about giving your child too much concentrated protein in a single dose, as an excess of any potentially allergenic protein could lead to a sensitivity to a particular food.

Most protein powders yield around 25 grams of protein per adult serving, which is too much for a toddler. The average toddler needs a bit over ½ gram of protein per pound per day. In fact, toddlers seldom have a protein deficiency.

Give your toddler one-third of the adult serving of protein powder, and mix it in a smoothie (see pages 7–8). An extra boost of a protein supplement in a smoothie is helpful during growth spurts and when recovering from ill-ness, when extra nutrition is required.

⅌

Thickening Formula with Food

Q *My mother wants me to add cereal to my eight-month-old son's bottle. She said she did this with me and enlarged the nipple hole so I could "drink my dinner." My pediatrician said, "No comment," when I asked her opinion. Is this a good idea?*

A In most cases, I do not advise adding cereal to infants' bottles. This older custom was used in an attempt to help babies sleep through the night (which it rarely does) or to space feedings further apart for the convenience of the parents. Nutritionally it is not a wise policy.

You have to understand that tiny babies have tiny tum-mies. They need small and frequent feedings rather than larger, widely spaced portions. Also, babies are used to drinking fluid through a nipple. Having to deal with a thicker, fast-flowing substance may confuse your baby while he's learning the difference between swallowing liquids and swallowing solids.

There is one condition in which thickening the formula with cereal is medically recommended. Babies who regurgitate food frequently often have a condition called gastro-esophageal reflux (GER), as discussed on pages 47–48. By taking advantage of the law of gravity, the heavier cereal-formula concoction may be regurgitated less.

If you have a healthy baby, it's best not to mix formula in any other way than the usual dilution recommended by the manufacturer. Your doctor may advise differently for medical reasons.

⌾

Healthy Eater vs. Glutton

Q *My two-year-old son loves to eat. He's not over-weight according to our pediatrician, but he relishes each bite of food. Sometimes I feel he's a glutton because he eats everything I set in front of him. Should I measure his food and hold back when I feel he has had enough calo-ries?*

A Oh, how many parents of picky eaters would love
to have your problem! It's important that your toddler
enjoy eating and enjoy food. But it's equally important
that he enjoy healthy eating habits and eating the right
foods. He probably has a lean body type that burns rather
than stores calories, which is why he is not overweight.
Genetically lean children tend to eventually work out a
proper balance toward eating the right number of calories
they need.

To make sure your child is getting a proper balance of
nutrients, serve him primarily nutrient-dense food. These
foods, such as eggs, fish, avocados, chickpeas, kidney
beans, lentils, tofu, tomatoes, whole grains, yogurt, flax
oil, and nut butters, pack a lot of nutrition into a small
number of calories. Avoid high doses of less-nutrient-
dense foods that provide minimal nutrition and a lot of
calories. This includes excessive juice (more than 12
ounces a day; dilute the juice at least 50 percent with
water), foods that have added hydrogenated oils (such as
packaged foods, cookies, and chips), highly sugared foods
(such as punch, sodas, juice drinks or "juice cocktail,"
marshmallows, and doughnuts). Stay away from fast-food
outlets as much as possible. If you do eat out, limit his
choices to foods that are not deep-fried in hydrogenated oil
(ask the restaurant server) or high in fat.

Remember, one of your main goals as your child's
home nutritionist is to shape his tastes toward a preference
for the most nutritious foods. And in addition to shaping
your child's tastes toward nutrient-dense foods, keep him
moving. Overeating along with lack of exercise is a serious

setup for obesity. Raise an active child to make sure those extra calories get burned off.

Also, monitor his snacks. While grazing is a normal and healthy eating habit, encourage him to snack on nutrient-dense, low-fat foods (like those mentioned above) rather than on high-calorie junk foods (prepared foods and packaged snack foods).

So enjoy your child's current eating attitude. If you want him to stay lean, don't put him on a diet, just monitor it.

✑

Solving Digestion Problems

Q *What does it mean if food comes out whole in my toddler's stools? When he eats raisins, corn, or grapes, they come out looking exactly the same as they did when they went in! Is he not digesting his food properly?*

A When it comes to food digestion, anything unusual that comes out at the bottom end reflects something amiss in what is going in at the top end. Normally, as food winds its way from mouth to anus it goes through a fifteen- to twenty-five-foot-long disassembly line, where nutrients are taken out of the food and absorbed into the blood-stream according to the body's needs. The excess waste is eliminated in the bowel movements.

If food is coming out the same as it went in, you're correct to assume that he is not digesting it properly. Either the intestines are "rejecting" the digestion of these foods or you are overwhelming the intestines with too much food too fast, and it can't digest them. Certain foods have what is called a rapid-transit time, meaning they go through the intestines too fast to be absorbed. These foods vary from person-to-person. It sounds like that is what's happening with your child.

Keep a diary of which foods appear undigested in his stools. These foods go on his list of rapid-transit foods—the ones he should temporarily eliminate or at least cut back on. Also, rather than letting him gorge on big volumes of food at one sitting, encourage him to graze on frequent mini-meals throughout the day. If he can eat half as much twice as often, you give his intestines a longer time to digest the food.

The foods you mentioned—raisins, corn, and grapes—are not the easiest to digest, especially if your child doesn't chew his food properly. Play a game with him that we call "Chew! Chew!" Show and tell him how to take smaller bites, and chew his food well and swallow it slowly. Chewing breaks up the fiber that holds foods together, especially foods like raisins, grapes, and corn. Chewing unwraps this tight food package so the digestive enzymes have easier access when breaking the food down in the intestines.

Also, the longer your child chews, the more saliva he

produces. Chewing and saliva help break down the food even before it reaches the intestines. An illustration that we use to teach our preschool children proper eating habits is a picture of a train winding its way from mouth to anus through the intestinal track. Show them how taking small bites, chewing food well, and swallowing slowly as the train takes off from the "station" allows the train to deliver the food more easily once it reaches the intestines. Using the train-journey analogy through the intestines will help your child understand why mother nutritionist "chews him out" for swallowing the food whole.

If your child doesn't have the patience to sit still and chew his food properly, make him smoothies, soups, and dips in which you have ground up the food for him. You'll be surprised that even those raisins and grapes that appear so frequently undigested in his stools will be digested once you liquefy them.

$\mathcal{L}\mathcal{D}$

Let's Play
Tea Party

Q *Whenever my mother comes to visit, she indulges my twin toddlers and lets them eat at their small table, using their plastic "tea set" dishes. The girls think it's wonderful and eat everything on their tiny plates—from spinach to fish. Personally, I think Grandmother is playing games with them and that they should join the family and eat with us each night. What do you think?*

A Smart grandmother! Sometimes games or tricks are necessary to get nutritious foods into your children with the fewest mealtime hassles. Let's face it—children get bored with the same mealtime routine.

Your mother's idea to change their dinner table to one their size certainly works, and it's one we have used many times in feeding our picky eaters. Having their own toddler-size table and utensils creates a toddlerlike ambiance that is likely to keep them sitting still longer during mealtimes. Think about how much having their feet dangle from too-high adult chairs encourages children to get up and run. With their feet planted firmly on the floor at the small table and chairs, your toddlers are apt to sit longer and stay focused on eating. Besides, this gives you more time to enjoy uninterrupted adult conversation with your visiting mother!

Don't feel you are losing control or spoiling your children by catering to their toddler cuisine. You are just being a wise and creative mother to let your "children be children."

✍

Like Father,
Like Son

Q *What do you think about my husband telling our three-year-old son to eat his vegetables while he refuses to eat them himself? It seems a bit hypocritical to me. Now my son has started refusing vegetables, saying, "Daddy isn't eating them either." How do I get Dad to lead the way with healthy nutrition so Junior will follow?*

A In many families, women have healthier eating habits than men. Perhaps this is one reason that nutrition-related diseases, such as heart disease and cancer, are higher among males.

To educate your husband and your toddler about healthy nutrition, you need to consider some creative marketing.

• *Buy nutritious food.* If your husband doesn't find junk food in your pantry or refrigerator, he's unable to eat it at home. By making junk food less accessible to your husband, you've already set the standard of what the family's nutrition habits will be. If your husband needs to satisfy his chip cravings, let him go out and buy chips himself. You will soon find that these trips to the neighborhood convenience store will become less convenient for him.

- *Make vegetable casseroles and vegetable dips.* Put his favorite food, such as a slab of steak or broiled pork chop, in the center of his plate. But surround it with multicolored vegetables (such as steamed broccoli florets, carrots, a seasoned tomato quarter, and dollops of sweet potatoes). Reduce the size of the meat on the plate and increase the vegetables, fruits, and whole grains.

- *Make a veggie pizza for the whole family to share.* Let your husband and toddler spend time cutting up favorite vegetables and creatively placing them on the pizza crust.

- *Take trips to family restaurants that have nutritious and attractive salad bars.* Encourage Dad to fill his plate with veggies and make an identical plate for your toddler (with smaller portions).

- *Make vegetable soups with some added chunks of beef, seafood, or chicken.*

- *Use herbs and spices to perk up the flavor of vegetables.* Choose from lemon juice, honey, dill, cinnamon, basil, nutmeg, garlic, oregano, curry powder, olive oil, sesame seeds, or grated cheese.

- *Make savvy salads using arugula, romaine, or spinach leaves.* These darker leaves are much more nutritious than the pale iceberg lettuce.

- *Roast vegetables in the oven.* Cut your favorite vegetables (yellow squash, zucchini, broccoli, onion, new potatoes, sweet potatoes, peppers) into chunks and place them on a cookie sheet. Drizzle olive oil on top and sprinkle with your favorite herbs, such as basil, garlic and onion powder, chives, parsley, oregano, rosemary, and salt and pepper. Bake in a 375° oven for one hour. Serve over pasta or rice and top with feta or Parmesan cheese.

Lastly, as only a wife can do, convey to your husband that because you love him, you want him to live longer. Shifting from a primarily meat-based diet to one that emphasizes vegetables and seafood is the best recipe for a healthy family.

ᘓ

Resources for Childcare Products and Information

Parenting and Pediatric Information

www.parenting.com. An informative Web site on parenting issues. Dr. Bill and Martha Sears answer parenting questions and host frequent chats and workshops.

www.AskDrSears.com. A comprehensive Web site on healthcare information for infants and children.

Baby Carriers

A soft baby carrier is one of the most useful parenting products you and your baby will enjoy. Consult the following resources for information on sling-type carriers and step-by-step instructions on using a sling.

The Original BabySling 800-421-0526 or
www.originalbabysling.com or www.nojo.com

Crown Craft Infant Products 310-763-8100 or
www.crowncraftsinfantproducts.com

www.AskDrSears.com Visit our store.

Bedside Co-Sleepers

A bedside co-sleeper lets baby and parents sleep close to one another yet still have their own space. This criblike bed safely attaches to the parents' bed.

Arm's Reach Co-Sleeper 800-954-9353 or
818-879-9353 or www.armsreach.com

Nursing Clothing and Accessories

Motherwear 800-950-2500 or www.motherwear.com

Breastfeeding Help and Resources

La Leche League International (LLLI)
800-435-8316 or 847-519-7730 or
www.lalecheleague.org

International Lactation Consultant Association (ILCA)
919-787-5181 or www.ilca.org

Corporate Lactation Program by Medela
800-435-8316 or www.medela.com

Attachment Parenting International
615-298-4334 or www.attachmentparenting.org

Mothering Multiples

National Organization of Mothers of Twins Clubs, Inc.
877-540-2200 or 615-595-0936 or www.nomotc.org

Index

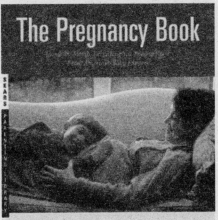